Men-at-Arms • 455

US Armed Forces in China 1856–1941

John Langellier • Illustrated by Mike Chappell

Series editor Martin Windrow

First published in Great Britain in 2009 by Osprey Publishing,
Midland House, West Way, Botley, Oxford OX2 0PH, UK
443 Park Avenue South, New York, NY 10016, USA
Email: **info@ospreypublishing.com**

Print ISBN 978 1 84603 493 0
PDF e-book ISBN 978 1 84603 894 5

Editor: Martin Windrow
Page layouts: Alan Hamp
Index by Sandra Shotter
Originated by PPS Grasmere: Leeds
Printed in China through Worldprint Ltd.

09 10 11 12 13   10 9 8 7 6 5 4 3 2 1

A CIP catalogue record for this book is available from the British Library

FOR A CATALOGUE OF ALL BOOKS PUBLISHED BY
OSPREY MILITARY AND AVIATION PLEASE CONTACT:

North America:
Osprey Direct, c/o Random House Distribution Center
400 Hahn Road, Westminster, MD 21157
E-mail: **uscustomerservice@ospreypublishing.com**

All other regions:
Osprey Direct The Book Service Ltd, Distribution Centre, Colchester
Road, Frating Green, Colchester, Essex, CO7 7DW, UK
E-mail: **customerservice@ospreypublishing.com**

Osprey Publishing is supporting the Woodland Trust, the UK's leading
woodland conservation charity, by funding the dedication of trees.

www.ospreypublishing.com

Artist's Note

Readers may care to note that the original paintings from which the
colour plates in this book were prepared are available for private
sale. All reproduction copyright whatsoever is retained by the
Publishers. All enquiries should be addressed to:

www.gerryembleton.com

The Publishers regret that they can enter into no correspondence
upon this matter.

US ARMED FORCES IN CHINA 1856–1941

INTRODUCTION

I N THE 18th century the Celestial Empire held vast treasures that were the envy of other nations. Tea, silk, and fine chinaware were among the luxury goods sought by Western traders to feed the insatiable markets of Europe and America; but China required almost nothing from these strangers, since the Dragon Throne ruled over a virtually self-contained domain and had little interest in mechanical toys. Precious metals, however, were acceptable: if the foreign barbarians paid in gold or silver they would be supplied with the exotic raw materials and products of the empire, though only while being kept at arm's length in terms of political and cultural relations.

As time passed the trade deficits in China's favor became enormous, and the drain on the coffers of other countries, particularly Great Britain, created such problems that Queen Victoria's government took measures to halt this one-way flow of specie. Impatient with the failure of diplomatic and economic avenues, Britain applied military leverage to open up China to foreign imports; other powers, including Japan, were not far behind, and eventually the United States followed suit. The foreigners pressed for the physical concession of coastal and river-port enclaves for traders, where they could operate in privileged independence of Chinese law and custom. As each decade passed during the 19th century more foreign naval forces appeared, much to the chagrin of China's rulers and population, while the protection of Christian missionaries provided a repeated excuse for landings and deeper penetrations.

One of the few products that found a ready market in China was the opium grown in Britain's colonies, and in 1839 open warfare broke out as the British tried to force China to accept this addictive and debilitating import. Nearly a decade after this First Opium War the British and French were in the forefront of another major test of arms between China and the Europeans. This Second Opium War or Arrow War erupted at a time when major internal upheavals threatened the ruling Ching (or Manchu) dynasty in Peking, thereby further eroding China's ability to protect herself. The Celestial Empire was militarily

US Navy Commander Andrew H. Foote, captain of the sloop USS *Portsmouth*, led a landing force of sailors and Marines in the capture of the Barrier Forts at the mouth of the Canton river in November 1856. The photograph was taken in later years, after Capt Foote had distinguished himself during the American Civil War. (LC)

A contemporary sketchmap of the area of northern China where US Army and Marine garrisons served for almost four decades following the Boxer Rising. Their essential mission was to ensure security along the railroad corridor between Taku at the mouth of the Pei Ho river, Tientsin, and Peking. Detachments rotated at various times though Tangshan (center) on the Peking–Mukden railroad north of Taku, and Chinwangtao (top right) on the coast just inside the Chinese-Manchurian border, at the end of the Great Wall. During the 1900 Relief Expedition the railroad from Tientsin to Peking had been torn up by the rebels, and the columns marched up roads close to the Pei Ho river as far as Tungchow due east of the capital, before turning west. General Chaffee's US contingent first saw major combat on August 6 at Yang Tsun due north of Tientsin, where the rail embankment and the river road come together. (USAHI)

antiquated, and from the mid-century onwards modern firearms were another commodity traded into China on a massive scale, including artillery for her coastal defenses. Not to be left out of the competition for Chinese markets, the United States, during its days of 'manifest destiny', also became a player in the game.

CHRONOLOGY

June 18, 1844 US Marines from USS *St Louis* come ashore in Canton to protect American citizens during a period of rioting, remaining through July 20.

October 23, 1856 Nineteen Marines and 64 sailors arrive from USS *Portsmouth* to protect Americans in Canton. Reinforcements arrive from USS *Levant* and the frigate *San Jacinto* on October 27 and November 12 respectively.

November 20, 1856 A combined Navy and Marine landing party attacks the 'Barrier Forts' on the Pearl river below Canton.

July 31, 1859 US Marines and sailors land from USS *Mississippi* to provide security for Americans in Shanghai during fighting between British and Chinese forces in the area.

June 22–25, 1866 After the American consul is assaulted, Marines and sailors from USS *Wachusett* land in a raid to capture the perpetrators.

July 14, 1866 The crew of USS *Wachusett* help fight a fire in Shanghai.

June 13, 1867 After a shipwrecked American merchant crew is murdered by locals in southern Formosa, Cdre Roger C. Belnap leads 180 Marines and sailors from the steam sloops USS *Wyoming*

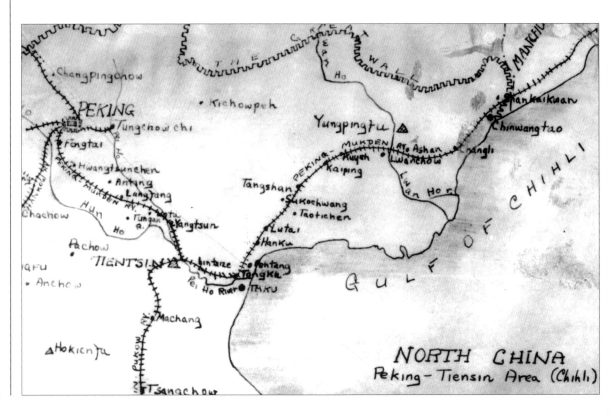

NORTH CHINA
Peking–Tiensin Area (Chihli)

and *Hartford* ashore, burning a village and killing townspeople.

March 25, 1894 Marines from the sidewheel gunboat USS *Monocacy* provide an honor guard for the Chinese viceroy's official visit to the US consulate in Tientsin.

November 4, 1898 Marines from USS *Baltimore, Boston*, and the cruiser *Raleigh* (C-8) arrive at Taku, then make their way inland to provide the first guard force for the American legation in Peking.

The Boxer Rising:

May 29, 1900 US Navy Capt Bowman McCalla and US Marine Capt John Myers set out from Taku at mouth of Pei Ho river to march to Peking via Tientsin, with Marines and sailors from USS *Oregon* and the cruiser *Newark* (C-1); the first contingents of other foreign marines and sailors arrive in Peking two days later.

July 10, 1900 Headquarters and one battalion of the US First Marine Regiment, plus an artillery company, land at Taku to be brigaded with two battalions from the Army's Ninth US Infantry.

July 29, 1900 US Army transport *Grant* drops anchor in Taku Bay with Gen Adna Chaffee aboard to take command of US land forces.

August 15, 1900 Foreign Powers Expeditionary Force arrives to lift the Peking siege.

October 10, 1900 US First Marine Regiment departs China.

September 12, 1905 Duty of US legation guard in Peking transferred from US Army to US Marine Corps; 100 Marines from the Philippines are detailed.

The fall of the Empire:

January 30, 1911 Revolutionaries in the middle Yangtze provinces establish the 'Literary Study Society' from the remnants of earlier secret groups. For the remainder of the year revolution and military mutinies intensify.

October 13, 1911 A battalion of 360 US Marines commanded by 15 officers leaves the Philippines for Shanghai as a reserve force during turbulent Chinese efforts to form a republic.

November 4, 1911 Two dozen Marines land from the cruiser USS *Albany* (CL-23) as a guard for a cable station in Shanghai.

November 29, 1911 The cruiser USS *Saratoga* (ACR-2) sets sail from Shanghai for Taku to provide security for American missionaries.

December 29, 1911 At the Nanking Conference the newly returned exile Sun Yat-sen is elected provisional president of the Chinese Republic.

January 10, 1912 General Orders No. 4 call for the 1st Battalion, Fifteenth US Infantry and a machine gun platoon to depart the Philippines for Tientsin.

March 10, 1912 Marines from the tender USS *Rainbow* (AS-7) begin a

1900: Officers of the Ninth US Infantry and other units (note the Engineer, center rear) enjoy a short respite as they sail to China; that regiment would suffer badly from sickness after they landed at Taku. Most wear the M1895 forage cap and the mohair-trimmed undress jacket with dark blue trousers; the officer at front left wears an M1883/90 'sack coat,' and the handsome figure at right rear a campaign hat, and sky-blue trousers confined by web leggings. (NARA)

two-month detail in Peking reinforcing the legation guard.

November 1912 Three dozen Marines from Guam take up position at Chefoo in defense of Americans.

1912 President Sun replaced by military leader Yuan Shih-kai.

1913 Failed rebellion by Sun Yat-sen.

July 7, 1913 Marines deploy from USS *Albany* at Shanghai, joined July 28 by reinforcements from USS *Rainbow*.

December 1915 Yuan Shih-kai declares himself emperor.

June 1916 Death of Yuan ushers in years of chaos as regional military leaders compete.

1916–30 The Warlord Period:

May 4, 1919 Post-World War I efforts by China to restore her territorial integrity are crushed by the Treaty of Versailles, provoking the May Fourth movement with the goal of retaking the country from foreign domination. Reorganization of Sun Yat-sen's Nationalist Party (Kuomintang, KMT) follows; Soviet advisors help KMT establish its own army from 1923.

July 1, 1921 Chinese Communist Party (CCP) is established in Shanghai by a leadership including Mao Tse-tung.

February 14, 1923 A detachment of Marines from the gunboat USS *Asheville* (PG-21) reports to Masu Island, where marauding bandits threaten US civilians.

November 16, 1923 A Marine detachment offers protection to American missionaries in Tunghan.

October 6, 1924 Marines from USS *Ashville* reinforced by 101 from the Philippines deploy to Shanghai, and the following month march on to Tientsin.

January 15, 1925 When a warlord's troops rebel in Shanghai a small detail of Marines from the gunboat USS *Sacramento* (PG-19) help to protect the International Settlement. Seven days later 140 more Marines shipped from the Philippines provide additional support through February.

June 5, 1925 Marines from USS *Huron* again land at Shanghai in response to violent outbreaks following death of Sun Yat-sen in March. On June 9 a commercial vessel lands a further party, which remains through August.

November 9, 1925 Marines take up positions in Tientsin.

December 30, 1925 Unrest in Shanghai once more brings Marines into the city.

November 12, 1926 Marines from the auxiliary ship USS *Gold Star* (AG-12) are posted to Chingwangtao.

February 9, 1927 A provisional Marine battalion from Guam is billeted in Shanghai. By February 24 the Fourth Marine Regiment disembarks from San Diego; it will remain in the International Settlement of the strife-torn city until 1941.

August 1927 Mutinies in Nationalist 11th Army lead to formation of first Communist units under Chu Te.

March 4, 1928 An American commercial vessel is recaptured from the Chinese by Marines and sailors from the cruiser USS *Pittsburgh* off Shanghai.

May 2, 1928 BrigGen Smedley Butler leads his Third Brigade headquarters, the Sixth Marine Regiment, and an air unit (VF-3M) into Shanghai to reinforce the Fourth Marines.

June 6, 1928 As Chiang Kai-shek takes his KMT forces north, Butler relocates his headquarters and Sixth Marines to Tientsin.

January 19, 1929 Disbanding of US Marines Third Brigade leads to withdrawal of its units from Tientsin.

September 18, 1931 The 'Mukden Incident' launches Japan's occupation of Manchuria.

Japanese aggression begins:

January 28–March 3, 1932 Proclamation of new Japanese puppet state of Manchukuo, with former last Chinese emperor Pu-Yi as head of state. Armies of Republic of China and Empire of Japan clash; the incident results in the demilitarization of Shanghai, and a prohibition on the Chinese government posting troops in their own city. During the conflict the Fourth Marines assume defensive positions in Shanghai.

February 1, 1932 The Thirty-First US Infantry regiment is ordered to Shanghai, arriving on February 4 to reinforce American forces there.

July 5, 1932 Thirty-First US Infantry returns to the Philippines.

January 1934 Marines from the gunboat USS *Tulsa* (PG-22) assume defense duties at the US consulate in Foochow during a period of concerted attacks by Chiang's KMT forces on the Communist Red Army. The Communists retreat and the Long March begins.

1937: July Battle of Lugou Bridge ('Marco Polo Bridge Incident') leads to eight-year Sino-Japanese War; Peking and Tientsin captured.

November Shanghai falls to Japanese; **December** Nanking captured by Japanese, leading to widespread massacres.

March 2, 1938 Battalions of Fifteenth US Infantry leave China after 26 years of duty in country.

August 8, 1938 The fall of Peking to the Japanese leaves the Marines of the US legation guard surrounded by the troops of an aggressive foreign power.

August 12, 1938 The Fourth Marines, with additional support from sailors and Marines from the cruiser USS *Augusta* (CA-31), take up defensive duties in Shanghai International Settlement once again. Seven days later they are augmented by 104 Marines from the Philippines.

November 28, 1941: the end of the 'China Marines.' Men of the Fourth Marines, in forest-green service dress and heavy marching order, pass through the crowded city streets in column of threes on their way to Shanghai docks for embarkation. Note the neatly blocked Montana-peak campaign hats on top of their old 'long packs.' (FVF)

August 26, 1938 Another company of Marines reports to Shanghai.

September 19, 1938 The Sixth Marines return to Shanghai along with the headquarters of the Second Marine Brigade.

October 1938 Japanese capture Canton.

December 12, 1938 Japanese sink the gunboat USS *Panay* (PR-5) on the Yangtze river.

February 18, 1939 The Sixth Marine Regiment and Second Marine Brigade headquarters withdraw from Shanghai.

February 28, 1939 200 Marines from the legation at Peking assume the vacated post at Tientsin.

November 10, 1941 Navy Department authorizes gunboats and Marines to be withdrawn from China.

December 7, 1941 The Japanese attack Pearl Harbor.

December 8, 1941 US Marine legation guards in North China stationed at Peking, Chinwangtao, and Tientsin surrender to Japanese forces, and became POWs for the duration of World War II.

BLUEJACKETS ASHORE, 1856

During the 1840s the United States had little involvement in China. By the following decade, however, anti-foreign resentment greatly increased during the country-wide chaos triggered by the so-called Taiping Rebellion and the eruption of the Second Opium War. During this period many Chinese viewed missionaries as spies and allies of the Taiping rebels, whilst Western merchants were detested as beasts preying on the Chinese people. In this climate of unrest the American consul at Canton requested US Navy Cdr Andrew H. Foote of the 22-gun sloop *Portsmouth* to provide a security force for his countrymen who resided in the area of this important port in the south of the country.

As day broke on October 23, 1856, four naval officers and 60 sailors, along with 2nd Lt William W. Kirkland and another 18 Marines, came ashore at Canton from the *Portsmouth*, which at the time was anchored 8 miles downriver at Whampoa. The landing party fanned out, taking up various positions to protect the American compound in Canton. Four days later the 20-gun sloop USS *Levant* brought reinforcements when a detail of sailors and Marines led by 2nd Lt Henry B. Tyler linked up with *Portsmouth*'s shore party. A minor incident took place on November 2 when the American sentinels clashed with Chinese troops, fortunately without casualties on either side. Over a week

The 22-gun sloop USS *Portsmouth*, whose sailors and Marines took part in the fighting for the Barrier Forts on the Pearl river at Canton in November 1856, alongside 'Bluejackets' and 'Leathernecks' from from the *Levant* and the *San Jacinto*. (LC)

later Capt James Armstrong steamed onto the stage aboard the 13-gun warship *San Jacinto* from Shanghai. Armstrong was now the senior American officer in Canton, and was charged with the security of a community of United States citizens whose unrest grew daily. On November 14 he ordered Brevet Capt John D. Simms and another 28 Marines to go ashore; Simms was to command the combined Navy-Marine landing force in Canton.

The American senior officers realized the danger for their small force, particularly from Chinese forts which stood between the squadron and the city. The shore party in Canton could only be supplied by a daring run up the Pearl river past the guns of these defenses, or by employing small boats under the cover of night. The situation seemed to improve when local Chinese leaders assured Armstrong that the Americans living in the area would be secure, and the captain recalled all but a small detachment of Marines who would remain on duty at the American compound.

On November 15, as the landing party returned to Whampoa, guns from one of the Chinese bastions lashed out at the Americans. Hostile bombardment resumed the next day, this time finding its mark and killing one of the men in a small boat Armstrong had dispatched to take depth readings in case the American ships had to make a run upstream. In response, at 3pm on November 16, Armstrong ordered *Portsmouth* and *Levant* to fire on the barrier forts, but the latter vessel ran aground, obliging *Portsmouth* to proceed alone. Within a half hour of setting sail the exchange of gunfire began, continuing until the light faded; one Marine suffered a critical wound and the ship took considerable damage.

Sickness then forced Armstrong to return to USS *San Jacinto*, leaving Cdr Foote in command. Evaluating the four daunting fortifications that opposed the US squadron, and believing that there were thousands of Chinese troops in the area, Foote decided that a preemptive strike was his best course of action. On November 20 he began with a naval bombardment to provide covering fire for a landing party of 287 officers and men, including Foote himself, 50 Leathernecks and a complement of Bluejackets all under Capt Simms in the vanguard. Securing a beachhead, the Americans rushed the rear of the first fort, dodging sniper fire as they made a swift, successful attack. The Chinese fled, and sustained many casualties as musket balls rained down on them from the walls they had just abandoned. Some of the survivors dashed to Canton city, 4 miles away, where news of the fort's fall prompted the Chinese to launch a counterattack to regain their outpost. A large body of Chinese troops made a series of assaults, but American musket and howitzer fire drove the attackers back.

With the initial objective in hand, the Americans pushed forward the next day to repeat the exercise against the second of the forts. Again the warships provided fire as the small boats landed Simms' command, which quickly gained its objective, and Cpl William McDougal from *Levant*'s US Marine detachment hoisted the US colors aloft. Captain Simms then set out to sweep the Chinese from the river in order to avoid a crossfire that

Re-equipped during the latter 19th century with imported heavy artillery like this Krupp gun, the Chinese forts at Taku represented an attempt to protect the nation from incursions into her ports and navigable rivers by the navies of the foreign powers, such as that at Canton in 1856. The attempt failed on June 17, 1900, when the allied navies avoided the seaward-pointing batteries by mounting their assault on the landward side by means of disembarked troops supported by small river craft which had already passed upriver beyond the Taku Forts. (GL)

'Boxers' photographed at Tientsin; note what appear to be red headscarves and armbands. These men seem to be unarmed; when they attacked the legations they carried broadswords and polearms – they usually disdained the firearms that they associated with the 'foreign devils.' The same was not true of the Imperial troops who supported them; the Tenacious Army of General Nieh Shih-cheng which resisted the allies at Tientsin had Mauser rifles, Maxim machineguns and modern artillery. (LC)

would complicate the attack on the third fort; the Chinese gun crews were caught off guard, and abandoned their pieces. Now only one enemy stronghold remained, and the following day it too capitulated. The Americans destroyed and disposed of the captured cannons to prevent their future use; and by December 5 the granite-walled forts themselves had been reduced to rubble with powder charges. After Armstrong's and Foote's rapid victory, an apology was delivered by the Chinese for the incident on November 16 that had triggered this series of exchanges.

Over nearly half a century the American residents in China enjoyed relative security, though local incidents occasionally prompted warships to disembark landing parties of sailors and Marines to retrieve threatening situations. The service became well practiced at such small-unit infantry tactics over the decades; however, at the turn of the century unrest on a much larger scale endangered the lives of US citizens and other foreigners residing in China.

THE BOXER MOVEMENT, 1900

At the conclusion of the Spanish-American War in 1898, America's acquisition of the Philippines both stimulated and facilitated a further interest in China. Merchants and missionaries from the United States joined the Europeans and Japanese who had appeared in increasing numbers during the latter half of the 19th century. The Manchu monarchy (still seen by many of their subjects as foreign occupiers themselves) had been almost bankrupted by the Taiping Rebellion and the years of regional warfare that had followed, and had been obliged to mortgage the government to the Western powers, which took over the running of the Chinese customs service and some other aspects of administration. A naval war with France in the 1880s had seen coastal forts destroyed and ports blockaded, and in the 1890s Japanese victories had forced China to cede both Korea and Formosa. These humiliating defeats, and the powerful and entrenched foreign presence that now extended far beyond mere trade, aroused Chinese fears of an actual partition of the country between the foreign powers.

Despite the voracious expansion of their so-called spheres of influence by these nations – particularly the Russians and Japanese – the American and British governments opposed the outright carving-up of Chinese territory. By September 1899 the United States announced that it had secured agreement from the interested powers to the maintenance of an 'open door' policy in their relations with China, exchanging increased access for a halt in moves toward outright colonization. This diplomatic maneuvering offered little comfort to many Chinese; even as the agreement was being proclaimed a grassroots militant movement emerged, vowing to drive the barbaric foreigners from the territory of the Middle Kingdom. Outrage grew over what was seen simply as the invasion and despoliation of their land, the degradation of their people and the destruction of their ancient ways of life.

A powerful reaction against these interlopers began in the northern part of the country headed by the Yi Ho Tuan movement, roughly translated as the 'Society of Righteous and Harmonious Fists'; outsiders came to call them simply 'Boxers,' in part because of the martial arts exercises that they practiced. Members of the Yi Ho Tuan adhered to a strict discipline, demonstrating their strength of will by following a special dietary regimen, and through their shadow-boxing training, coupled with other rites, the adepts of this cult could achieve a trance-like state. To impress gullible potential recruits the Boxers might fire a blank matchlock musket at one of their members, declaring that true believers were impervious to bullets. The Yi Ho Tuan prophesied a renewal of past glories through the expulsion of the Westerners; they succeeded in gathering a following of tens of thousands in the countryside, not least by promising that once the invaders had been driven out the rains would return and crops would spring forth – a seductive claim in times of drought and famine. The Boxers dubbed the foreigners, including missionaries, as 'primary devils,' but they also attacked Chinese Christian converts as 'secondary devils.' Striking in the northern provinces first, in December 1899 they killed the first Christian missionary. Violence against foreign residents and Chinese Christians soon spread from Shantung and moved towards Peking, where Boxers torched a railroad station – a hated symbol of the industrial nations that were brazenly coming to seize control of China.

The increasing size and dominance of the Boxer movement worried the precarious Chinese central government in the Forbidden City. Civil war threatened the ruling Manchus once again, yet there were some who saw a use for this martial society, and chief among them was the Dowager Empress Tzu Hsi. This remarkable woman would have impressed Machiavelli with her decades of deft and ruthless political machinations. Secretly sympathetic to the Boxers (as were some of her closest advisors), she hoped that the movement could dislodge the invaders from China without explicitly implicating the Imperial government. Cautiously and secretly, the empress encouraged and aided the Boxer cause.

The Peking Legations
Prior to this point, life in the foreign legations clustered in Peking had been safe and far from arduous. For example, the British minister in Peking, Sir Claude MacDonald, enjoyed a salary of 5,000 pounds per annum that allowed him to live

Map of the foreign legation quarter at Peking, 1900. The 'Purple City' (top left) is the Forbidden City. The defended perimeter in late June is shown by light dotted lines, and the lines of 'Xs' denote the shrunken perimeter of mid-August. The Tung Pien gate, originally allocated to Gen Chaffee's contingent of the relief force, is off the map to the right at the eastern end of the outhern wall of the Tartar City; since it was 'stolen' by the Russians, the sector of eastern wall they actually climbed was north of the Tung Pien. (*Behind the Scenes in Peking*)

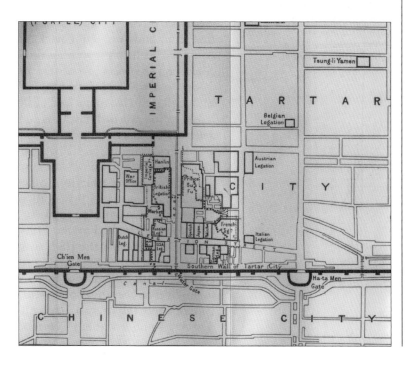

The reality: Capt John 'Handsome Jack' Myers, commander of the US Marines who helped defend the Peking legations. (*Behind the Scenes in Peking*)

handsomely, and most of the Westerners dwelling in and around the legation quarter – which stood in the shadow of the Forbidden City to its west and north – lived in some luxury in commodious compounds. Their residences contrasted sharply with the smaller Chinese structures on the outskirts of the enclave. Cheap labor, imported luxuries, and a constant cycle of social events made life enjoyable for the diplomats, bankers and other assorted businessmen who lived there with their families. This comfortable existence lulled many into a false sense of security; even as the destruction of property and the killing of more 'devils' continued in the countryside, Sir Claude assured alarmists that the foreign legations in Peking would be the last places that need fear attack, since this would expose the imperial government to the direct vengeance of the foreign powers. Not everyone succumbed to the fairytale atmosphere of the Chinese court and the legations, and, fearing an onslaught, several of the foreign ministers in Peking requested that armed guards be sent from their countries' fleet units on the coast of northern China. They cabled requests for 550 troops, and on May 31, 1900 an allied force arrived by train. A report in the New York *Herald* the following month stated: 'The marines of the English, the Russians, the Japanese, and the French all came up the day before yesterday from Tientsin, and when they were finally landed at Pekin, there was great excitement as to which body of marines should lead.' US Navy Capt Bowman McCalla, who commanded the USS *Newark*, gained that honor when he led his men into the legations at the double-quick.

Although McCalla brought the Americans into Peking, it was Capt John 'Handsome Jack' Myers of the US Marine Corps who commanded this force. Myers' detachment consisted of 25 Marines from USS *Oregon*, and another 23 Leathernecks, three Bluejackets, one chief machinist and one hospital apprentice from USS *Newark*, recently landed from Nagasaki, Japan; the arrivals also included Capt N. H. Hall USMC from that ship, and Asst Surgeon T. M. Lippitt, US Navy. The contingent, equipped in heavy marching order but without baggage, had left the *Newark* on the morning of May 29. Myers noted that his were the first troops to arrive in Tientsin, where the foreign residents received them with delight. His force left again at 4.30pm on Thursday May 31, reaching the railroad terminus outside Peking at about 11pm that night. They carried 9,720 rounds of ammunition in their belts, 8,000 more for a Colt machinegun, and 10,000 in boxes, totaling 27,720 rounds. They also packed only five days' rations and two large ship's breakers of water.

Fifty-five of the American officers and men would help defend the legations alongside 82 British Royal Marines, 81 Russians, 51 Germans, 48 French, 35 Austro-Hungarians, 29 Italians and 25 Japanese. Support weapons were limited to one British Maxim machinegun and an almost useless Nordenfeldt, the US Marines' Colt .236cal 'potato-digger,' and a 1-pdr Italian quick-firer with just 120 rounds. Of the 473 civilians present, about 75 had prior military service, and another 50 or so armed themselves as best they could with sporting guns to man the barricades (where their improvised bayonets earned them the nickname of the 'Carving Knife Brigade.') This motley force of just over 500 armed men protected about 125 noncombatant civilian men and nearly 150 women and 80 children, plus some 2,700 Chinese Christians who had taken refuge in the missions and the legation quarter. This had an irregular perimeter butting against the southern wall of the area known as the Tartar City; standing north of the Chinese City, this enclosed the Imperial and inner Forbidden City. The legation compounds were divided by the Imperial Canal running through the Water Gate.

On June 2, Capt McCalla and two other naval personnel returned to Tientsin. On June 6 the Boxers cut rail communication and burned many stations, and Capt Myers wired Tientsin for at least 25 more men; the next day he recorded that 'there having been no plan for common defense adopted by the officers commanding the various guards, the English marine officer, at my request, called a meeting of all the officers, and it was decided that at the first sign of an outbreak all the noncombatants together with all provisions, should be sent to the English legation; and that all streets leading into the legation quarter should at once be barricaded, no Chinese being allowed to enter without a pass.'

On June 9, Boxers attired in their red headscarves, wrist-streamers and sashes assaulted the Peking racetrack, the first foreign target to be struck in the city, and in the legation quarter the efforts to bolster defenses became more urgent. The British missionary Jesse Ransome wrote that sandbag barricades would eventually extend to 'include all, or nearly all, of the foreign Legations, and our Legation'– the large British compound forming the northwest corner of the perimeter. She went on: 'The Russians and Americans who adjoin us [to the south] are to come in here if hard pressed, as we are most defensible. At present all looks quiet within the city, but they say the whole country outside is in a perfect ferment.' Ransome claimed that the work of fortification involved 'every man, woman, and child… exposed places are defended by piles of sand-bags,' and on almost every roof piles of bags made from every conceivable material from the poorest burlap to the richest silk were stacked to provide cover for the sentries. 'There are several bomb-proof shelters made; but, so far, the enemy have not been able to touch any but the upper storeys with bombs. If, however, they can force the Americans from their post on the [south] wall, they would simply command this compound, and would fire bombs into it as hard as they liked.'

She recorded the shared concerns within the legations that 'every Mission compound and foreign house outside the lines' would be put to the torch, 'with the exception of a great Roman Catholic church and compound in the North City, which is defended by foreign soldiers [sic], and the Methodist Episcopal Mission, which is being defended by American troops.' The latter had been garrisoned on June 8, at the request of US Consul Edwin Conger, who dispatched ten men under a corporal as a guard for the American missionaries and their flock at this exposed position. The following day

The fantasy: in the 1963 Allied Artists Pictures epic *55 Days at Peking* Charlton Heston played 'Maj Matt Lewis,' seen here receiving dire news from Paul Lukas portraying a German doctor. (GL)

Myers provided reinforcements when more refugees poured into the Methodist mission from Tungchow and outlying districts of the city; Capt Hall and another ten Marines were detailed to this cluster of buildings, which lay on a small street about three-quarters of a mile east of the legations. Similarly, the French Northern Mission (Pei T'ang Cathedral) some distance from the main compounds provided rudimentary protection for the French nuns and priests along with their Chinese converts, and was guarded by some 40 French and Italian sailors.

Meanwhile, as hopes of a peaceful resolution dimmed, Sir Claude MacDonald sent a plea for a relief force to Admiral Sir Edward Seymour at Taku on the coast. On June 11, Imperial Chinese soldiers killed Chancellor Sugiyama of the Japanese legation, and this brazen murder convinced even doubting foreigners and Chinese Christians of their precarious position, prompting a flight into the legation quarter. On June 16 the Boxers burned a large sector of the Chinese City which included many businesses catering to foreigners. Three days later the ministers received a warning from the Dowager Empress' representatives that the court could no longer ensure the safety of those in the legations, and a demand for their immediate evacuation. The diplomats refused to be intimidated, and sent a request for an audience to the Chinese foreign ministry. When they received no reply the Western and Japanese representatives assumed that they had no option but to prepare to defend themselves, in the hope that a relief column would soon come to their rescue.

On June 17 a messenger sent out the previous day by the Americans had returned with a report that an estimated 30,000 Boxers and Chinese soldiers had halted an allied relief column at Huangsun, and other rumors placed it at Tientsin. Its arrival was critical, since Manchu officials friendly to foreigners were hard pressed to maintain the Imperial Army's neutrality; according to the British eyewitness Oliphant, this was due to the fact that Americans and Russians were prone to fire at any Chinese who came into view wearing 'a bit of red in his uniform, under the idea that he is a Boxer.' The mood of the Imperial troops was confirmed on June 20 when the German minister Baron von Ketteler, insisting on making a visit to the foreign ministry, was stopped and shot dead by an Imperial soldier. That afternoon the Chinese in the streets and buildings surrounding the foreign compounds opened fire.

The siege
On June 21 the Austrian Capt von Thomann unilaterally declared himself in command of the defense, but the following day he panicked and ordered the abandonment of the outer perimeter; luckily this order was countermanded before the Chinese could exploit it, and MacDonald was appointed to command in von Thomann's place. Japanese and German marines made successful sorties on the 24th, and on June 25 Deaconess Ransome reported 'furious fighting on the City Wall during the day.' This was held by the US Marines, who advanced almost as far west as the Ch'ien Men gate to the Forbidden City to neutralize a cannon. Ransome's diary continued: 'The night between Saturday and Sunday was one of incessant tumult; the Chinese took to sending bombs, and one burst in the room where two English people were sleeping. The whole force of the compound was turned on to making sand-bags to strengthen our position.'

On July 1, Americans and Germans on the perimeter came under a heavy crossfire from the Ch'ien and Hata gates. When three Chinese field pieces were trained on their position they retreated northwards from their barricades into the British Legation, bringing the Colt machinegun. Soon after 10am reinforcements were dispatched under Capt Myers to retake the abandoned posts, although only

US Marines, British Royal Marines and a sailor crewing the 'International' gun, contrived from odd components by ingenious defenders of the legations. (*Behind the Scenes in Peking*)

the US sector was regained. Shortly thereafter a Royal Marines captain and ten men arrived to bolster Myers' detachment. Two days later a further foray was mounted to protect the approach to this vital southern sector; for some inexplicable reason the Chinese had been left unhindered to build a barricade immediately adjacent to the American sector, later erecting a 15-foot tower from which their riflemen could rake the defenders from short range.

On July 3 the British memoirist Oliphant volunteered to accompany 15 Americans, 26 British and 15 Russians in a sortie led by Capt Myers. That officer addressed them in words that struck Oliphant as being 'utterly unlike what a British officer would have said under similar circumstances... saying that we were about to embark on a desperate enterprise, that he had himself advised against it, but the orders had been given, and we must do it or lose every man in the attempt.' Myers then briskly explained the plan: to 'line up on the wall and rush the covering wall just under the tower, and then follow up that covering wall till we got to the back of the Chinese barricade.' While the objective was straightforward, Myers' concluding remarks must have chilled many in the ranks when he ordered that 'the wounded must be left lying until the barricade was taken, and finally, that if there was anyone whose heart was not in the business he had better say so and clear out.' In response one man claimed to have 'a sore arm, and went down'; the rest of the troops stood their ground, although they 'showed no violent alacrity in lining up in the front rank of those who were to vault over the barricade.'

The Americans and British were to go to the left, while the Russians were to take the right-hand barricade and attack the top of the ramp occupied by the Chinese. Oliphant's diary records that 'the British and Americans all mixed together... scrambled and dropped down the ten feet on the other side.' The tower appeared to be unmanned, but nevertheless Myers became the first casualty when he 'tripped on a Chinese spear which was lying in the grass, and got a nasty flesh wound in his calf,' which prevented him from participating in the charge. The left flank assault succeeded, but when Oliphant reported to Myers for further orders he learned that the Russians had turned back half way. The American captain told him that 'we must certainly clear the back of the barricade and then occupy the east side of it. I returned accordingly, and we cleared out the back of the barricade, which was easy enough, as all those who were not dead had fled.' The wounded Myers handed over command of the American contingent to his fellow Marine Capt Newt T. Hall, who led them from July 3 to July 21 during a time of considerable combat.

On July 7 an old rifled cannon barrel was found by a trench-digging gang, and a couple of US Marines lashed up a usable weapon on a carriage with spare Italian gunwheels. Some previously useless Russian 9-pdr shells were disassembled into separate charges and projectiles, and were found to be an approximate fit when loaded via the muzzle. On the 8th Jesse Ransome wrote: 'They thought at first it was Chinese, but it turns out to be English make, and they think it may be one of those we brought up in 1860. The engineers made a carriage for it, and this afternoon they fired some Russian bombs from it three or four times. It seems to have only had the effect, however, of stirring up the enemy, for they have been shelling us vigorously; one shell hit the house, and another burst close to the hospital.' Manned by Americans, the cannon came to be known by many names: The International, Old Betsy or Puffing Betsey, Boxer Bill, Old Crock and the Dowager Empress. This hybrid weapon symbolized the diverse nature of the allied defense force, and the makeshift means they were forced to adopt in order to survive under almost constant fire and occasional assaults by several thousand Chinese, both Boxers and elements of the Imperial Army. The beleaguered legation quarter had dwindling supplies of food, medicines and ammunition, and on July 13 an explosion under the French Legation killed several Bluejackets, heralding a new phase of mining and counter-mining.

In his report of the fighting during July, Capt Hall singled out one of his men for praise: 'I respectfully invite the attention of the commanding officer to the courage and fidelity of Daniel Daly, private, US Marine Corps, at all times, and to his conduct on the night of the 15th of July, 1900, when he volunteered to remain alone in the bastion under the fire of the enemy while I returned to the barricades for the laborers.' His heroic act contributed to Daly being recognized by the legendary Smedley Butler, a Leatherneck officer who served against the Boxers and who returned to China in command of a brigade more than a quarter of a century later; Butler pronounced Daly 'the fightingest Marine I ever knew.'

Captain Hall's period of leadership coincided with the US Consul's summation of the situation in Peking. In a dispatch sent by messenger to his counterpart in Tientsin he relayed: 'Have been besieged in British Legation five weeks under continual fire of Chinese troops but since 16th by agreement there has been no firing; 50 marines of all nationalities killed and more wounded. We have provisions for several weeks, but little ammunition. If they continue to shell us as they have done, we can't hold out long, complete massacre will follow.' From July 17 to 25 there was in fact a mysterious and apparently spontaneous ceasefire at the barricades; after two more days' fighting a second, official truce lasted until August 4, but this did not halt attacks on the Pei T'ang Cathedral, where artillery and mines killed many.

On July 18 the Japanese minister received a report that a 12,000-strong relief force was gathering at Tientsin, and on August 3 Capt Myers – now in hospital with typhoid – received a coded message that 'ten thousand United States infantry and a body of cavalry' were making their way to Peking, while Japanese and British troops were engaging strongly entrenched Chinese at three places between Tientsin and the capital. The impossibility of timely two-way communications made such messages painfully frustrating; meanwhile, the mining and counter-mining continued.

THE RELIEF EXPEDITION

The Taku Forts and Tientsin

In fact, the 12,000 men led by the British Adm Seymour had been making their way to Peking since June 9, but made only slow headway; the under-rationed force became bogged down by inadequate transportation, and by stubborn resistance from the Boxers in tandem with Imperial troops. Once Seymour quit Tientsin to drive inland, the Boxers occupied the Chinese city there and put pressure on the International Settlement, while at the Taku Forts defending the mouth of the Pei Ho river Imperial forces seemed to be preparing to bar the waterway. Securing the rear lines of the relief force was obviously essential, and the allied commanders planned an assault on the powerful forts from the landward side with supporting fire from small gunboats sent upriver. This took place on June 17, with complete success.

At the International Settlement in Tientsin, meanwhile, a multi-national garrison of some 2,400 were holding a perimeter nearly 5 miles long (skilfully planned by one Herbert Hoover, the future President of the United States) against an estimated 10,000 Boxers and Imperial troops. Assaults began on June 17, but the garrison held out until the arrival on June 23 – at the second attempt – of an 8,000-strong relief column from Taku. The Imperial forces fell back towards Peking; on June 26 a patrol from Tientsin linked up with Adm Seymour's blocked force, which returned to that city. The Chinese town was still occupied, and it was July 14 before it was cleared after intense fighting. At last the allies could prepare for a second attempt to reach Peking, although this was delayed for some time by a rumor that the legations had already fallen to assault and massacre.

Officially titled the China Relief Expedition and under the interim command of the British LtGen Alfred Gaselee, a force of some 19,000 troops set out from Tientsin for the 70-mile march to the capital on August 4. The largest contingent were 10,000 Japanese (Gen Yamaguchi), with 4,000 Russians (Gen Linivitch), 3,000 British and Indian Army troops, 2,000 Americans, 800 French and small parties of Germans, Italians and Austrians, supported by 70 pieces of artillery and machineguns.

The US contingent was commanded by a former Frontier cavalry officer, MajGen Adna Chaffee; its main units were the rather sickly Ninth US Infantry led by LtCol Charles A. Coolidge, and (subsequently, after a delayed arrival from Manila) six

There is a suitable air of haste about this shot of men of the Fourteenth US Infantry boarding a transport in the Philippines to join the international relief force in northern China. Both khaki uniforms and blue shirts can be seen. (GL)

companies of Col A. S. Daggett's fitter Fourteenth Infantry; the Ninth provided most of the 200-plus infantrymen who were reported by the surgeons as unfit for duty and who remained at Tientsin. There were also two battalions of Marines, under Maj Littleton W. T. Waller and Maj William P. Biddle respectively; Light Battery F, Fifth US Artillery under Capt Henry J. Reilly, and assorted engineers, signalmen and medical personnel. The Sixth US Cavalry, whose horses had not arrived, remained behind together with a 100-strong Marines company, to assist the civil government of Tientsin; all Army troops in the city were put under the command of LtCol T. J. Wint, Sixth Cavalry. (On August 9, Capt De Rosey C. Cabell would catch up with the marching column with his Troop M of the Sixth, numbering two officers and 76 enlisted men.)

The only American ground transport in Tientsin at this time were 19 wagons, four ambulances, and nine Dougherty wagons belonging to the Ninth Infantry; fortunately a pack train became available just in time to provide logistical support for the American column. These means of transport were vital, since the Yanks carried only limited ammunition and one day's rations in their haversacks, while a four-day food supply and 100 rounds per man were hauled in wagons. Another ten days' rations were packed in junks that were to follow the army up the Pei Ho river; however, the energetic Maj Waller had managed to secure Chinese carts and packs sufficient to carry four days' rations for the Marines, thus relieving by that amount the pressure on the wagon train. Chaffee authorized a generous number of Chinese porters for each company, to carry cooking utensils, water, the litters for the sick and wounded, and other items for which it was impossible to make room on the wagons.

Pei Tsang and Yang Tsun

Early on the morning of August 5 the relief force came up against an estimated 10,000 to 12,000 Chinese who were en-trenched at Pei Tsang, but by noon the Japanese and Russians had driven them from their positions and out of the town. On the 6th, at Yang Tsun about 10 miles further on, it was the turn of the Americans and British, who were advancing under their heavy marching packs through choking dust in temperatures that rose as high as 104 degrees Fahrenheit. After an early morning halt the Americans resumed the advance north-wards on the river road, with the British on their right flank. Their route of march took them towards the embankment of the wrecked railroad; this converged with the river road about a mile and a half short of Yang Tsun, and at

US troops load carbine racks with .30-40cal Krags and .38cal Colt double-action revolvers – the issue weapons of the Sixth US Cavalry. Note that even as early as 1900 one soldier (second from left) has cutomized his M1899 campaign hat from the regulation fore-and-aft crease to a Montana peak. (GL)

that point the Chinese were discovered occupying the section immediately in front of the bridge and the bend in the road. In consultation with LtGen Gaselee, and at his request, Chaffee placed the Fourteenth Infantry to attack along the west side of the railroad, where they connected with the British line; the Russians were at

this time to the left rear of the British, probably in column. Chaffee crossed to the east side of the railroad embankment with the Ninth Infantry, Marines, and Reilly's battery, and deployed to support the march of the Fourteenth Infantry and British troops; Gaselee had lent a squadron of British cavalry to operate on their right flank.

While deploying to advance with the Fourteenth Infantry, Chaffee came under Chinese artillery fire from his right flank, and soon thereafter the commander of the British squadron reported eight companies of Chinese infantry and three guns in a village directly to Chaffee's right. It was clearly unsafe to leave his right flank exposed to such a force, and Chaffee directed a move against it; American guns soon silenced the enemy artillery and set the village afire. While moving toward it Chaffee received messages from the British commander requesting that American artillery should be brought to bear on the embankment and a village being attacked by the British and the Fourteenth Infantry, whereupon 'I abandoned the movement on the village with the artillery and marines, which were on the left, and at once changed direction of the battery and marines and moved toward the bridge or village being attacked by the Fourteenth and the British.' Artillery fire and infantry volleys were being delivered from various villages to the Americans' right and front. Notwithstanding Chaffee's reluctance to change the line of battle before accomplishing the cleaning out of the villages on his right, he went into position to assist the Fourteenth, intending to fire over the 20-foot-high railroad embankment.

The battery had unlimbered and was about to open fire when Chaffee saw men of the Fourteenth mount the embankment directly in its line of fire. He ordered his artillery not to fire, and within a minute thereafter the battery was fired upon by Chinese infantry or dismounted cavalry secreted in the cornfields within short range. The American gunners responded with shrapnel and, with the aid of the arriving Marines, dispersed this force. The Ninth Infantry, which in part came up to the right of the battery, mistook the Chinese flag for a French tricolor and withheld their fire, losing an opportunity to inflict serious damage. (Previously Gaselee had warned Chaffee to be careful not to fire on the Russian or French troops, indicating that they were likely to pass his front. In fact neither of these contingents was anywhere in advance of the American line or of the left of the British line, but the warning had been passed on to American regimental and staff officers and in consequence all troops hesitated to fire on unidentified bodies of men.)

MajGen Adna Chaffee (center, front) wears the khaki uniform with colored facings – for a general officer, dark blue – adopted soon after the outbreak of the Spanish-American War in 1898. Most of the officers of his staff wear variations on the 1899 pattern, with branch-color facings limited to the epaulets. (NARA)

The Fourteenth assailed the Chinese with vigor, supported on their flank by the British, who were intermixed with the Fourteenth because of the obstructed ground. In this attack the Americans suffered seven killed and 57 wounded, many falling victim to the fire of British and Russian batteries after the former Chinese position fell (a mishap typical of multinational operations reliant on primitive communications). The advance of the Fourteenth Infantry ended at the railroad embankment. The Ninth Infantry, Marines and the American artillery continued to advance northward through the villages lying to the east of Yang Tsun until they nearly reached the northern end of the city, where opposition practically dispersed. Chaffee withdrew his troops to camp near the railroad bridge.

Meanwhile, that same morning the Japanese had taken possession of Tungchow some 20 miles further north, and had pushed beyond it; there was now about 12 miles to go before they reached Peking. The eight powers then agreed that on August 13 they would engage in a reconnaissance in force. The Japanese would reconnoiter two roads on the right (north) of a canal and a paved road; the Russians would probe up the paved road, if at all; the Americans would push forward on a road just south of the canal; and the British on a parallel road about one mile to the left of the Americans. On August 14 the contingents would concentrate on the advance line held by the Japanese, and that evening a conference would be held to determine the method of attack on Peking; LtGen Gaselee hoped for a calmly coordinated final advance on the 15th, with each contingent attacking its assigned gate in the city wall without any competitive jostling.

Peking

Consequently, on the morning of August 13, Chaffee reconnoitered the road to be occupied by the Americans with Troop M, Sixth Cavalry, followed by Reilly's battery and the Fourteenth Infantry, up to the point about 7 miles west of Tungchow specified in the plan. Encountering no opposition, he directed the remainder of his contingent to close up on this advance guard, which they did at around midnight. The other forces had also reconnoitred their roads, and in view of the progress achieved it was agreed to bring the final assaults forward by 24 hours. However, while the other contingents bivouacked the Russians pressed ahead alone, and during at the night of August 13/14 heavy firing was heard from the direction of Peking. The Russians had attacked the Tung Pien gate at the eastern junction of the walls of the Chinese and Tartar Cities (previously allocated to the Americans) rather than their assigned

Tong Chih gate. Heavy artillery and small-arms fire continued throughout the night, and at daybreak the American, Japanese and French contingents broke camp and advanced, while confused staff officers tried to ascertain the relative positions of the different forces.

Chaffee ordered Capt Cabell and his Troop M forward on reconnaissance, and they had been absent no longer than an hour when a courier raced back to inform Chaffee that Chinese cavalry had surrounded the American horse soldiers. The general immediately ordered a battalion of the Fourteenth Infantry forward, and after about a mile and a half they found Troop M occupying some houses and firing from the roofs on a village to their front. After persuading the wandering French battalion to give him the road Chaffee joined Capt Cabell; he continued the reconnaissance to his front, wishing to get as near the wall of the city as he could but not expecting to move his whole force, which would be contrary to the plan agreed. Without serious opposition the Americans arrived at the northeast corner of the Chinese City; at about 10am Chaffee saw the advantage of holding the ground that he had gained, and directed his whole force to move forward. The Russians had made only limited progress at the Tong Pien gate, but by this time it was clear that the plan to act in concert was in tatters, and LtGen Gaselee had no realistic option but to order an immediate general advance.

General Chaffee decided to attempt scaling the high city wall between the Sha Huo and Tong Pien gates. Musician Calvin P. Titus of the Fourteenth Infantry volunteered to exploit a dead angle in the Chinese defenses, using holes where bricks were missing to clamber up the 30-foot wall at a partially sheltered point. When Titus reached the top he found the section unguarded; he dropped a rope, and soon about 20 other American soldiers had joined him. At just after 11am they raised the Stars and Stripes aloft; a ladder was quickly improvised, and by about noon enough Americans were up to take in the flank the Chinese defenders of the Tong Pien, allowing the Russians to clear it. Private Titus' bravery would be recognized by one of the 56 awards of the Medal of Honor made to United States servicemen for their conduct during this campaign.

Meanwhile, the Japanese blew in two gates through the eastern wall of the Tartar City, and British easily breached their assigned Sha Huo gate. They moved swiftly to the legation quarter where, just after 2.30pm on August 14, Indian soldiers of the 7th Rajputs broke through a barricaded canal sluice gate from the outside to be greeted by US Marines tearing it down from the inside. The 55-day siege had been lifted, but at a cost of at least 33 American dead and another 178 wounded. In all the defenders of the legations had suffered 64 military (including 7 Americans) and 12 civilians killed, and 156

Photographed after hostilities ceased in Peking, the Ninth US Infantry and Sixth US Cavalry parade outside the Sacred Gate. The troopers wear khaki tunics and breeches, the infantrymen blue shirtsleeve order with their light field kit in horseshoe rolls. (LC)

military (including 10 Americans) and 23 civilians wounded. Deaths among the Chinese refugees are unknown, but were certainly in the high hundreds.

GARRISONS, 1900–1941

At a conference held the afternoon that Peking capitulated the allied commanders decided not to occupy the Imperial City, and Chaffee withdrew the bulk of his troops to the previous night's campground, though leaving men to hold a position at the Chien gate in the south Tartar wall. British correspondent Henry Savage-Landor recorded what happened next: 'The Americans were at first encamped under the Tartar wall, where they baked in the boiling sun and suffered from lack of water. Then they were shifted to one of the courtyards of the Imperial City – a most unsuitable place – then again, much to the soldiers' delight, into the Temple of Agriculture,' across the main road from the Temple of Heaven, which was garrisoned by other foreign troops. Here, at what Savage-Landor maintained was 'the first sensible camp which the poor American boys had so far had in the China campaign,' the weary warriors could find some relief among 'shade from trees, green grass, and two magnificent wells of delicious water.'

However, the correspondent's further comments paint Chaffee in unflattering colors: 'General Chaffee seemed ever unnecessarily harsh and inconsiderate towards his men. It was understood that he had refused permission to his officers to take possession of the many magnificent Chinese tents, abandoned in their flight by the Imperial soldiers, both in the Imperial precincts and under the Tartar wall.' Supposedly, dozens of these 'enormous canvases, each well able to shelter twenty or thirty men' were there for the taking, but by Chaffee's orders they were 'left to rot in the mud and become sleeping places for pariah dogs, while his soldiers, ninety per cent of whom or thereabout were down with dysentery, fever, sunstroke, or other complaints, were suffering terribly from the drenching storms a night; no clothes to change, no blankets, and no shelter of any kind.' This exposure would become even more damaging with the arrival of cold weather, as the Americans had 'no winter clothing, nor prospects of receiving any, and within a few days it would be getting very cold at night.' Savage-Landor recorded American ingenuity when the troops produced 'funny little shelters with umbrellas, rags, silks, and Chinese cloth or matting, and gradually collected furs, which they used as bedding. The camp, especially in sunlight, had quite a picturesque appearance, but when heavy rain fell looked as miserable and wretched a place as one could gaze upon... They [literally] slept in pools of water.'

While the US troops hunkered down in Peking, several months of allied mopping-up operations followed in the provinces. President William McKinley's administration opted to refrain from participation, wishing to return most of the American troops to the Philippines before the winter clamped down. The Marines departed for the Philippines in October; a few detachments of limited size remained in China for several years, but by 1905 the Boxer scare had faded into history, and in fall that year the United States government withdrew the last Army troops from Chinese territory. For nearly a decade (with one important exception) the presence of the United States flag in China would be limited to US Navy warships occasionally dropping anchor briefly in one of her ports. The exception was the return in September 1905 of 100 US Marines, to assume a limited but highly visible role in the Chinese capital. Rather than battling Boxers this small Legation Guard force now led a more leisurely and routine life of urban ease, during which they gained a reputation for spit-and-polish.

US Army, 1912–1938

This placid posting would be disturbed when the Manchu imperial dynasty finally collapsed in fall 1911, ushering in 40 years of bloody turmoil across the vast expanses of the country as the Chinese Republic struggled to be born and to survive. A mutiny by Chinese troops around Hankow and Wuchang in October 1911 led quickly to the abdication of the last emperor, the boy Pu-yi, and the declaration of a republic under Sun Yat-sen. The first outbreak prompted the United States to invoke

A polyglot group of officers of the allied garrisons clustered around Tientsin, including several from the Fifteenth US Infantry, which first shipped to China in 1912 at the time of the turmoil following the fall of the Manchu dynasty. The officers of the different national units provided each other with a shared social life in this far-flung posting; identifiable in this group are the uniforms of the USA, Great Britain, France, Italy, Germany, Austria-Hungary, Russia and Japan. The photo is from the collection of Capt Garrison McCaskey of the Fifteenth. (GL)

In the aftermath of the Boxer Rebellion, 'buffalo soldiers' of the Ninth US Cavalry make preparations to depart for China from San Francisco as part of the occupation force. (LC)

Summer 1927: Doughboys from Company I, Fifteenth US Infantry march through Lung Su south of Tientsin in their field uniforms, including World War I vintage puttees and M1912 'Montana peak' campaign hats. (NARA)

the 1901 Protocol; 70 more Marines reinforced the Legation Guard during late November, and a small battalion was shipped from the Philippines to provide security at Shanghai and other ports. The crisis also brought the US Army back after more than six years of absence, to protect American interests in northern China at this time of violent unrest.

In early January 1912 the US War Department ordered the transport *Logan* with the 1st Battalion and Machinegun Platoon of the Fifteenth US Infantry to sail from the Philippines, and the unit arrived at Chinwangtao on January 18. They were dispersed at important stations, bridges and other key points along the railway, and from March 3 – in response to rioting, looting and burning of missions and other property – 200 of the approximately 500 infantrymen were detailed to Peking. This posting was of short duration, since Marines from USS *Abarerda* and from Taku relieved the temporary Army force between the 8th and 11th of that month. Nevertheless, the Fifteenth Infantry's headquarters staff, 3rd Battalion, quartermaster, medical, signal, band and other support elements were transferred from the Philippines, and soon after landing at Taku this force established a presence in the Tientsin area that would last for the following 26 years. The Fifteenth Infantry and its supports would function as a self-contained, balanced formation like the regimental combat teams of World War II (though much more lightly equipped). The infantry unit was the backbone of an American military presence that would vary in size over the years between 600 and 1,400 servicemen, and the Fifteenth's assignment would establish much of the regiment's tradition (including a motto derived from pidgin English, 'Can Do').

Service with this regiment was unlike that in any other United States infantry unit of the era, and had undoubted advantages. Chinese civilian employees performed nearly all fatigue duties, and cheap, expert laundry and tailoring allowed the troops to cut a dash. The food was excellent; during the 1920s – in contrast to Prohibition-era America – liquor was inexpensive and plentiful; and female companionship was readily available. During the summer each of the battalions took turns rotating through a four- to six-week summer camp on the beach near Chinwangtao; this location provided the

(continued on page 33)

1: Commander, US Navy; undress, 1856
2: Private, US Marine Corps; field dress, 1856
3: Corporal, USMC; Formosa, 1867

1: Corporal, USMC; undress, 1900
2: Private, USMC; campaign dress, Peking, 1900
3: 1st Lieutenant, USMC; campaign dress, 1900

B

1: Captain, US Navy; shore-going undress, 1900
2: Musician, 14th US Infantry; campaign dress, 1900
3: Private, 5th US Artillery; campaign dress, 1900

1: Major-General, US Army; Peking, 1900
2: Corporal, 14th US Infantry; winter dress, 1900/01
3: First Sergeant, 6th US Cavalry, c.1900

D

1: Battalion Sergeant-Major, 15th US Infantry; full dress, 1912
2: 1st Lieutenant, 15th US Infantry; full dress, 1912
3: Lieutenant-Colonel, 15th US Infantry; undress, 1912

E

1: Color-Sergeant, 15th US Infantry; summer service dress, 1912
2: Chief Petty Officer, US Navy; summer shore party uniform, 1917
3: First Sergeant, 15th US Infantry; walking-out dress, c. 1930

F

1: Pfc, USMC Mounted Detachment; Peking, c.1933
2: USMC winter cap badges, c.1935
3: Major, 4th US Marines; service dress, winter 1935/36

1: Able Seaman, US Navy Yangtze Patrol, 1930s
2: Campaign medals
3: Captain, 4th US Marines; Shanghai, summer 1937

2a

2b

2c

2d

space for rehearsing field problems, target practice, sightseeing at the Great Wall, and more. Of those days one officer recalled that 'soldiering was interesting and pleasant and not drudgery, even prideful.'

During its quarter-century in China the Fifteenth worked closely with British, French, Japanese, Italian and (until 1917) Russian units also stationed around Tientsin and at other points along the Chingwangtao–Tientsin–Peking railroad axis, all fulfilling the main mission of providing route security between the coast and the capital. For the first decade of deployment the China Expedition occupied fairly rudimentary facilities in Tientsin, but during World War I, when the German garrison was ousted from China, the Americans took over the former German barracks. During the years between the world wars the War Department redesignated the command twice: first in 1924, as American Forces in China, then five years later as US Army Troops in China. While the organization of the Americans changed from time to time the assignment to China proved relatively calm, although the continuing state of chaotic warlord rivalry, Communist revolution and civil war over much of south and central China might threaten the north at any time and required the garrison to remain alert to developments.

At the end of the 1920s, with the Nationalist Kuomintang's 'Northern Expedition' advancing slowly from the south and bringing the civil war closer, recommendations to the War and State Departments proposed that the Fifteenth should be withdrawn from China because its mission no longer seemed appropriate. The unit was serving in a highly exposed and isolated position, which even at the best of times taxed logistics and training. This view was shared by many of the regiment's successive commanders (including, perhaps, George C. Marshall, the future chief of staff of the US Army during World War II). With a limited number of troops and little weaponry heavier than small arms, the Fifteenth would be no match for an enemy that managed to acquire modern heavy weapons, armor and aircraft. Luckily, despite years of opportunistic meddling in China by foreign governments and arms suppliers, none of the parties to the continuing civil wars came to pose such a threat; but from late 1931 the expansionist forces of the Empire of Japan emphatically did.

In November to December 1931 the successful invasion of Manchuria to the north by the Japanese Kwangtung Army gave much food for thought; and the urgency of the American position was underlined in January – May 1932 by the so-called 'Shanghai incident,' when that city was bombed and four-plus Japanese divisions landed to attack the Kuomintang's 19th Route Army defending it. During this major emergency the Thirty-First US Infantry (1,056 all ranks) was

Men of Company K, Fifteenth Infantry break for chow on the Taku Road in the late 1920s. Note the regiment's distinctive unit insignia just visible on the front of the campaign hat – kneeling man, second from left. (NARA)

shipped to Shanghai from the Philippines to help protect the International Settlement, which found itself a close spectator to all-out war; the regiment remained there from February through July 1932, but its defenses were not tested.

The desire to extract the Fifteenth Infantry from China became even more pressing following the 'Marco Polo Bridge incident' of June 7–8, 1937, when Japanese forces attacked and rolled over Chinese forces on the outskirts of Peking. When they captured Peking and Tientsin on June 30–31 the US garrison found itself isolated in an active war zone, thus compromising its neutrality and effectively terminating the regiment's security mission. On March 2, 1938 the Fifteenth Infantry and its support units sailed for the United States, to return to their native soil at Ft Lewis, Washington.

1927: a battalion review of the Fifteenth Infantry at the American Barracks in Tientsin. Note the company guidons, in blue with white crossed rifles between the regimental number and company letter. The soldiers wear khaki summer service dress but with the olive drab vizored caps of the M1926 uniform. (NARA)

A souvenir of a prized posting for US Marines with a taste for the exotic coupled with home comforts; the Legation Guard enjoyed a traditional American-style Christmas meal. (GL)

US Marines, 1927–1941

The Fifteenth Infantry's duties paralleled the responsibilities of their brothers in arms serving with the US Marines. Although isolated landings at Shanghai and other coastal points had been necessary at various times since 1911, it was in 1927 that the Navy Department began a concerted troop buildup on Chinese soil; this would eventually consist of the Third Marine Brigade, with some 4,400 officers and men commanded by the hard-as-nails BrigGen Smedley Butler, directed to Shanghai from San Diego, California. The first wave consisted of the Fourth Marines, a two-battalion regiment, stationed at Shanghai from March 1927 through November 28, 1941. In March 1928 the Fourth was joined by the Sixth Marines, an aviation element and the Third Brigade headquarters, which all moved up to Tientsin in June. However, the brigade was disbanded and its units at Tientsin were withdrawn in January 1929.

Before 1932 the only excitement the Fourth Marines got was healthy competition on the sports fields with other American and foreign units stationed in China, but this changed in a hurry when Sino-Japanese hostilities broke out in the Shanghai area. On January 27, 1932 the International Settlement there proclaimed a state of emergency, and all foreign troops took up defensive positions. The Fourth Marines, totaling

Christmas Greetings
1925

Marine Detachment
American Legation Guard
Col. L. McCarty Little
Commandant

PEKING   CHINA

1,247 officers and men, were among those placed on alert, and they were reinforced by other USMC elements including shipboard detachments from the fleet anchored in port, details from the Legation Guard in Peking, and other Marines who sailed from Manila during the first week of February, thus increasing the Fourth Marines' strength to 1,694 all ranks. The presence of the Leathernecks was important to the morale of the Shanghai International Settlement, the foreign enclave where thousands of diplomats, businessmen, and their families lived in a luxurious but at times precarious situation sealed off from the life of the country. Although the Settlement was on Chinese soil it was governed by an international municipal council; while the Shanghai Volunteer Corps had come into being as a sort of multinational militia to protect the foreign residents, in reality the only real security was provided by the modest garrisons of European and United States soldiers, Marines and sailors.

The fighting around the city ceased in May after a successful Chinese defense, but while Chiang Kai-shek's Kuomintang armies continued to battle the Communist guerrillas the Japanese military were preparing for outright invasion of China. In July 1937 the manufactured excuse of the 'Marco Polo Bridge incident' brought major Japanese forces racing into northern China, capturing the capital and fanning out to the west and south. On 13 August the Japanese landed 10,000 troops near Shanghai, beginning a savage three-month battle for the city. When intense fighting broke out in the Chapei district north of the city center and south of the Yangtze its proximity to the International Settlement prompted Col Charles F. B. Price, who commanded the Fourth US Marines, to confer with American consul general Clarence Gauss and MajGen A. P. D. Telfer-Smollett, who commanded Britain's small Shanghai Area Force. Although Price cooperated with other foreign officers he was subordinate to Adm Harry E. Yarnell, the commander of the US Asiatic Fleet, and the admiral ordered Price to repel by force any attempt by either Chinese or Japanese forces to breach the American sector.

On November 12 the city finally fell to the Japanese after 92 days' fighting; neither side had forced combat on the cordons around the International Settlement, but the Japanese strongly desired to occupy the European and American enclaves in the captured port. Outright seizure was out of the question, but indirect methods were tried. For example, on December 12, 1937, Japanese aircraft sank the USS *Panay*, killing two crew members and wounding others; while this belligerent action incensed the United States, an apology from Japan along with cash reparations kept the two countries from conflict. Almost simultaneously with the sinking of the *Panay* the Japanese asserted that they would hold a victory parade in Shanghai that would pass through the International Settlement, over the objections of the municipal council. During the course of this controversial show of triumphalism a Chinese national lobbed a grenade that killed three Japanese soldiers and wounded three policemen. While the perpetrator was shot on the spot the Japanese used the incident as a pretext to comb though the international enclaves to uncover more 'assassins,' and even contended that they would have to assume control to maintain order. Colonel Price responded robustly, making clear that any attempt to implement this plan would not be tolerated. Thereafter tensions ran high in Shanghai.

A corporal of 'China Marines' displays the standard USMC blue dress uniform, with the white 'cover' worn for warmer seasons; see also Plate G1. (GL)

In contrast to smart dress blues, the everyday summer dress for Marines in China in the 1930s was the khaki shirt and trousers with the olive campaign hat. (GL)

Even more vulnerable hostages to fortune were provided when, in early 1938, just 50 Marines from the Peking Legation Guard were moved to Tientsin to maintain a token presence in a station now being abandoned by more than 1,200 Army personnel; another 20 were sent to Chinwangtao, the traditional debarkation site for Leathernecks reporting to China. However, appeals to withdraw the dangerously small US Marine presence from China fell on deaf ears until late November 1941. Finally, on the 27th–28th of that month, the Fourth Marines were withdrawn from Shanghai to the Philippines, but this escape offered only a brief respite. Barely a week later Pearl Harbor was bombed, and many of the American soldiers, Marines and sailors reassigned from China soon faced overwhelming odds when 57,000 Japanese troops invaded the islands later in December. Most died or were captured during the next five months, and more would perish during the infamous 'Bataan Death March' and the years of unspeakable treatment as prisoners of war that followed the US capitulation in May 1942.

The fate of the 203 US Marine Corps personnel who had remained behind in northern China was forlorn. Their departure from the country had actually been planned for December 10, 1941, but the Japanese preemptive strike on Pearl Harbor made this impossible. On the morning of December 8 the Marine executive officer at Tientsin, Capt John White, learned of the bombing from a radio communiqué.

He reported it to his commanding officer, Maj Luther Brown, and almost immediately Brown received an ultimatum from the Japanese calling for his men at Tientsin and Chinwangtao to lay down their arms by 1pm that afternoon. Brown contacted his superior in Peking, Col William A. Ashurst, and asked for orders; realizing that resistance would be suicidal, Ashurst instructed him to surrender, despite the fact that some of his Marines were prepared to go down fighting. All the USMC personnel passed into captivity, as the proud days of the 'China Marines' came to an end.

Just ten days before the attack on Pearl Harbor, the band of the Fourth Marines paraded through the streets of Shanghai for the final time. (FVF)

The Asiatic Fleet, based in the Philippines, was the parent command for the South China Patrol before World War I, when this study of the USS *Galveston*, USS *Bainbridge* and USS *Saratoga* was taken off the coast at Chefoo. After 1918 the riverine force was retitled the Yangtze Patrol. (USN)

THE 'BROWN WATER NAVY'

The history of the China Marines regularly intersected with that of their parent service, the US Navy. From 1854 onwards American naval patrols sailed the major rivers giving access to inland cities, and particularly the Yangtze, the great commercial waterway that snakes across the whole breadth of southern China linking the cities of Chunking, Hankow and Nanking with the sea at Shanghai. These craft, tasked with protecting American lives and American interests, formed part of the East Indies or later Asiatic Squadron until 1907, when all USN ships in the Pacific came under the Pacific Fleet. Three years later the Asiatic Fleet came into being, headquartered at Manila in the Philippines; under its control, a flotilla of gunboats evolved into the South China Patrol, in turn retitled the Yangtze Patrol Force after World War I. By the 1930s this force numbered eight vessels on regular riverine duty, with periodic offshore support from destroyers, light cruisers, and even an occasional battleship from the US Asiatic Fleet.

The 1920s

The crews of the Yangtze Patrol did not always find their deployment routine, and in several instances they took part in heated small-scale actions. For example, they were particularly active during 1923 at the height of the 'Warlord Period', when Sun Yat-sen's Kuomintang government based at Canton in the far south was struggling to establish its Republican government, while the central regions were wracked by chaotic banditry and piracy in the gaps between the fiefs of such figures as Wu Pei-fu ('the Jade Marshal') and Sun Ch'uan-fang ('the Nanking Warlord'). The junior officers commanding US Navy gunboats found themselves obliged to engage in diplomacy to defuse threats, and not only to the mission stations and commercial interests who were their primary responsibility. During 1923 one of the Yangtze Patrol commanders brought together representatives of the generals from two opposing armies to negotiate a truce that prevented the bombardment of a large and populous city, which was garrisoned by one of the warlords and surrounded by the forces of the other. For his part in averting great loss of civilian lives by arranging this truce and the withdrawal of troops from the city without bloodshed, the naval officer received the warm thanks of the city officials.

When necessary the gunboat crews had to take more forceful action. One incident that same year involved the passenger steamer *Alice Dollar*, which was saved from destruction or capture after it was fired upon by several hundred bandits. Also in 1923, boarding parties secured and returned to the American owners many junks loaded with oil that had been captured by pirates. The year ended in further complications when in December 1923 the Sun Yat-sen government threatened to seize the customs houses and wharves in Canton, which had long been under international control. In concert with other nations the United States sent six destroyers to Canton; this show of force and cooperation by the various naval powers compelled the president to rescind his threat, and the customs continued to be administered as formerly.

Apart from the operational and political challenges faced by junior officers on the spot, who sometimes had to make life-or-death decisions that might have diplomatic repercussions, their everyday duty involved demanding tasks of seamanship and navigation as they sailed far up rivers with swift currents and unpredictable shallows. The old gunboats with which the patrol was equipped in the early 1920s needed replacement with more suitable vessels, and the Navy Department asked Congress for funds to construct six new river gunboats. In the meantime, to augment the old gunboats in service on Chinese rivers, the minesweepers USS *Penguin* and *Pigeon* were placed in commission on October 13, 1923 at Pearl Harbor and proceeded to the Asiatic Station for duty in the lower waters of the rivers – their draft was too great for them to penetrate the upper reaches. Washington responded positively to the request following urgent appeals for greater protection of American shipping and trade in China, and for more adequate police protection for American missionaries in unstable areas.

Even before construction of the six new craft was completed the safety of American lives and

Over much of the vast expanse of China the roads were rudimentary, and historically the river and canal system had provided a major element of the transport network. Watercraft of every size plied the rivers, from seagoing junks in the lower reaches through small sampans on the creeks. Since the rivers were the major routes of penetration for trade, and the interior was periodically unsettled and lawless, American commercial operations – as well as the many mission stations – looked to the US Navy patrols for protection, particularly along the mighty Yangtze which bisected the country. This photo of US troops on supply junks dates from 1900 on the Pei Ho, in the dawn of a 40-year US presence on China's waterways. (LC)

property in the vicinity of Shanghai and the lower Yangtze was threatened in September– October 1924 by the operations of the contending armies of 'the Jade Marshal' and 'the Tiger of the North,' Chang Tso-lin, in the so-called Second Chihli-Fengtien War. Available vessels of the Asiatic Fleet, reinforced by US Marines from Guam, once more came to the rescue. Acting with other powers, they kept the lower Yangtze open for navigation and prevented the fighting reaching Shanghai. Year after year US Navy reports chronicled similar episodes, involving large roving bands of former soldiers and bandits who periodically fired on United States warships and merchant vessels along the Yangtze. This necessitated the continued maintenance of a convoy system and of armed guards aboard American merchant vessels.

The 1930s

In summer 1927 the mutiny of elements of the Nationalist army saw the birth of the first Communist revolutionary units under Chu Te and Mao Tse-tung. The last independent warlords were now passing from the scene, but the prolonged civil war between the Kuomintang under Chiang Kai-shek and the Communists, soon complicated by the Japanese invasion of Manchuria in 1931, added to the Navy's burdens. One annual summary succinctly stated that 'China continues in a state of disruption with internecine strife and communist-bandit activities now engaging the wholesale attention of the Government forces.' Finally, Japanese expansionism led to anti-Japanese demonstrations and boycott activities in the larger Chinese cities and ports. These outbreaks frequently endangered American lives and interests, and further demanded the presence of US Navy vessels in unsettled parts of the country.

Besides providing security to American citizens and their property, the Navy also occasionally extended humanitarian aid. In 1931 the Yangtze Patrol, augmented by destroyers of the Asiatic Fleet and by USS *Houston*, flagship of the commander-in-chief, cooperated with United States consular officials at Hankow and Nanking, rendering assistance and standing by to evacuate United States nationals after summer floods – judged to be the worst disaster on record in China – submerged an estimated 34,000 square miles. Final estimates put the number of Chinese lives lost in this natural catastrophe at 150,000 or more, and the property losses reached $500 million. The Patrol provided what aid it could to the masses of homeless Chinese who had fallen victim to nature's wrath.

With the so-called 'Marco Polo Bridge incident' of July 7, 1937, the previously intermittent hostilities between the Kuomintang forces and the Japanese Kwangtung Army based in Manchuria spiraled into all-out war, and US Navy gunboats came to the rescue of another group of civilians. The US State Department ordered the evacuation of American citizens from Nanking, the capital city of Generalissimo Chiang Kai-shek, which was threatened by the Japanese advance later that year. The Bluejackets gathered up and steamed away with those fellow countrymen who decided to flee war-torn China; others, including missionaries and doctors, chose to stay, and were witnesses to the horrific 'Rape of Nanking' after the city fell to the Japanese in December 1937.

Over the next four years the US Navy maintained an uneasy presence along the coast and the Yangtze river. Fearing the worst, the senior naval officer responsible for China, Adm Hart, communicated with his superiors that he favored 'the withdrawal of all our armed forces,' contending that 'in the event of war with Japan they would be quickly contained or destroyed, probably without being able to inflict even a comparable loss on the enemy.' Late in 1941 word came from on high that the Yangtze Patrol, then consisting of USS *Oahu* and *Luzon*, should depart from its China station in November; so too would USS *Mindanao*, the South China Patrol flagship. Conversely, USS *Wake* stayed behind as a station ship in Shanghai for support of the American consular communications, and USS *Tutulia* would remain in Chungking, the new capital of the Nationalist government and Chiang Kai-shek's headquarters, where American diplomatic and military missions would be based through World War II. Even so, the remaining presence was purely representative rather than having any operational capability, and it was with the departure order of November 1941 that US Navy duty afloat and ashore on the China station came to an end after nearly a century.

'FLYING TIGERS'

Before the Navy sailed away one last quasi-American unit would inextricably link its fate to that of China. In late April 1937, Capt Claire L. Chennault, an outspoken US Army Air Corps officer who had been retired from active duty on health grounds the previous year, bid farewell to his wife and seven children at their home in Louisiana and set out for China. There, at the request of the politically active Madam Chiang Kai-shek, he accepted a confidential three-month mission to provide a succinct, honest survey of the status of the Chinese Air Force. His findings were less than encouraging; at the end of his tour he reported to the generalissimo that less than 100 Chinese aircraft were airworthy. This crushing news came at a desperate hour, when the Chinese had reached

the point of no return in efforts to reach a peaceful resolution to the Japanese encroachments into their sovereign territory – encroachments in which greatly superior numbers of Japanese aircraft flown by combat-experienced crews had played a crucial role. The Chinese appealed to Chennault to take on the daunting task of training their air force, and during this period he also flew many dangerous sorties against the Japanese. During the summer of 1937 some relief came from an unexpected source when the Soviet Union dispatched six squadrons manned by Russians to fight the Japanese, and also provided 400 aircraft for the Chinese Air Force. This reinforcement helped forestall Japan's achievement of air superiority, but the Chinese still lacked sufficient numbers of up-to-date machines and trained pilots of their own to achieve any longer term success.

The best-known movie depiction of the work of the Yangtze Patrol was 20th Century Fox's *The Sand Pebbles* (1966), filmed in Taiwan and Hong Kong from Thomas McKenna's best-selling novel of the same name. Set in 1926, it starred Steve McQueen (right) and Richard Attenborough (left) as two ill-fated petty officers. (GL)

November 1941: wearing foul-weather ponchos against the rain, US sailors and Marines depart for the Philippines aboard the transport *Merry Moller*. Many of these men would die or be captured resisting the Japanese invaders during the early months of 1942. (FVF)

In the summer of 1938 Chennault arrived in Kunming, the capital of Yunnan province in western China, and soon thereafter formed an international squadron of foreign bomber crews; a number of Americans served in this short-lived unit. In late 1940 Chennault returned to the United States, and with US government approval he ultimately secured 100 Curtis-Wright P-40B fighters from the Buffalo, New York factory (the type known to the British Royal Air Force and later more generally as the Tomahawk). These fighters would equip three Chinese squadrons; all were to mount a pair of .50cal machineguns in the nose, while the wing guns would be 7.92mm Colts for two of the squadrons and .303in Brownings for the third. To find the required pilots and ground crews, some of Chennault's comrades set about recruiting in the United States, with the knowledge and blessings of American authorities; they secured 59 flyers from the US Navy, 33 from the US Army and seven from the US Marine Corps. Those who signed on as pilot officers would supposedly be equivalent to US Army Air Corps first lieutenants, paid $600 a month, while more experienced flight leaders deemed equal to Army captains would be paid $675; the three squadron leaders ranked as Army majors at $750 a month. Regardless of rank, all were to be given a $500 bonus for each Japanese plane they downed. Besides pilots, nearly 200 other Americans would be brought in to serve in varied capacities from ground crews to medical personnel, and even a chaplain.

The First American Volunteer Group was formed on August 1, 1941; on that day Order No. 5987 signed by Generalissimo Chiang Kai-shek made the unit an official element of his Nationalist forces. During its first months of existence this organization was stationed in Burma, during which time several of the original members resigned or were killed in the course of their training for active duty. The first to fall, John D. Armstrong, crashed during mock aerial combat on September 8, 1941. Others would follow, and these losses required replacements. For instance, on November 12 a contingent arrived from the United States that included a pugnacious former Marine first lieutenant named Gregory Boyington, later to achieve fame with his 'Blacksheep Squadron' during the war in the Pacific; he would record his first six aerial victories with the AVG. Another member of the group was

The outbreak of the Pacific war ensured almost immediate movie fame for Chennault's American Volunteer Group, the first US flyers to meet the Japanese in battle. Republic Studios' *Flying Tigers* (1943) provided John Wayne with one of his many screen roles as a World War II hero. (GL)

Charles Bond, who is credited with suggesting that a shark's-teeth motif should be painted on the deep air scoops under the noses of the AVG fighters; when this was tried, one of the pilots remarked approvingly that it 'looks mean as hell.' Other distinctive markings were added: the 1st Squadron adopted a green apple over which a naked Eve chased a uniformed Adam, the 2nd chose a black-and-white Chinese panda, and the 3rd applied nose art of a red nude with a halo and wings, taking the nickname 'Hell's Angels.'

The AVG's more popular collective nickname of 'Flying Tigers' arose from a December 29, 1941 *Time* magazine article entitled 'Blood for the Tiger.' This told the story of the unit's first combat encounter when flying from Kunming, China, where most of the group had been transferred shortly after Pearl Harbor. According to the article, on December 20 pilots of the unit shot down four of ten Japanese bombers spotted about 30 miles south of the city. From that day forward the Flying Tigers would enter the annals of aviation history. Many of the original members of the AVG would remain in service throughout World War II, serving both in the China, Burma, India (CBI) Theater and elsewhere; in 1942 the AVG was incorporated into the US 14th Army Air Force based in China, with General Chennault in command.

SELECT BIBLIOGRAPHY

Biggs, Chester M., Jr, *The United States Marines in North China, 1894–1942* (Jefferson, NC; McFarland & Co Inc, 2003)

Bodin, Lynn F., *The Boxer Rebellion* (Oxford; Osprey Publishing, 1989)

Cornebise, Alfred Emile, *United States 15th Infantry in China, 1912–1938* (Jefferson, NC; McFarland & Co Inc, 2004)

Ford, Daniel, *Flying Tigers: Claire Chennault and His American Volunteers, 1941–1942* (Washington, DC; Smithsonian Books, 2007)

Harrington, Peter, *Peking 1900: The Boxer Rebellion* (Oxford; Osprey Publishing, 2005)

PLATE COMMENTARIES

A1: Commander, US Navy; undress, 1856
The US naval officer's winter undress uniform consisted of a navy-blue double-breasted frock coat ornamented with gilt buttons, and matching trousers. Rank insignia for a commander included shoulder straps bearing crossed silver anchors on a background bordered in gold embroidery. The dark blue cap likewise bore crossed silver anchors, enclosed in a gold embroidered wreath and mounted above – for this rank – three gold lace bands. The sword was the M1852, with a black leather scabbard set off by gilt fittings.

A2: Private, US Marine Corps; field dress, 1856
The US Marines' regulation field uniform comprised a large, soft-crowned forage cap like that worn by the Army since 1825, identified by large brass letters 'USM'; and a short sky-blue kersey 'roundabout' jacket with matching trousers – the shade naturally faded with use and washing. Whitened crossbelts made from buffalo hide supported the 40-round M1842 cartridge box and the socket bayonet, but an additional narrow waist belt had started to appear early in the 1840s; sometimes this replaced the bayonet belt, sometimes it was worn over both crossbelts. Percussion-lock conversions of smoothbore flintlock muskets, like this old M1816 Springfield, were newly issued in 1856, and required an additional small pouch for the percussion caps.

A3: Corporal, US Marine Corps; Formosa, 1867
On June 13, 1867 the Marines from the USS *Wyoming* and *Hartford* formed part of a landing party sent ashore in southern Formosa in response to the murder of American merchant seamen. Their M1859 uniform included a kepi-style forage cap now bearing a brass bugle-horn badge, its curl surrounding a silver Old English script 'M' set on a red leather backing. The single-breasted dark blue frock coat had seven brass front buttons and two at the rear of each cuff; all ranks had a line of scarlet piping around the base of the stand collar, and NCOs were identified by yellow tape chevrons on scarlet backing, worn points-upward on each upper sleeve. The sky-blue wool uniform trousers were replaced with white cotton in hot weather. The standard weapon was the M1863 Springfield rifled musket. Slung on the left hip are a tarred canvas haversack and a clamshell-shaped tin canteen covered with cloth.

B1:Corporal, US Marine Corps; undress, 1900
The Marines who landed from the battleship USS *Oregon* and cruiser *Newark* wore either campaign hats or this forage cap – based on the Army's M1895 – bearing the corps' eagle, globe, and anchor device. The M1892 uniform consisted of a navy-blue tunic with red piping; the sky-blue trousers bore an inch-wide red sidestripe for NCOs, and the chevrons were unchanged. The dark blue web ammunition belt with suspenders supports leather single-clip pouches for reloading the 6mm bolt-action M1895 Lee rifle, ordered by the Navy Department instead of the Army's Krag-Jorgensen. The other item of field equipment is the pair of tall brown canvas leggings, laced up the outer sides.

B2: Private, US Marine Corps; campaign dress, 1900
The drab felt campaign hat was adopted in 1898, and was usually worn creased fore-and-aft; the eagle, globe and anchor badge was fixed to the left side of the crown, and a narrow leather chinstrap could be passed up through holes on each side of the brim to run around the front of the crown. Removing the undress jacket in the heat of battle, a Marine enlisted man could fight in the dark blue flannel pullover shirt, which had two large button-through patch pockets. The Lee cartridge belt is worn here without suspenders; those visible are supporting the trousers.

B3: First Lieutenant, US Marine Corps; campaign dress, 1900
The officers' M1875 undress tunic was still regulation at the time of the China Relief Expedition; this surviving example is trimmed and corded with khaki rather than black mohair braid. The rank of first lieutenant is indicated by a single silver bar on the front of each side of the collar, ahead of the silver USMC device, which is also displayed on the left side of the crown of the 1898-pattern campaign hat. Note the officers' one-and-a-half-inch scarlet stripes on the trouser outseams, and the Mameluke-style Marine officers' sword.

C1: Captain, US Navy; shore-going undress, 1900
Blue or white uniform and cap-covers were worn according to season. The navy-blue cap has a black ribbed mohair band, a large bi-metal badge, and – for this rank – embroidered gold leaves around the vizor. The M1877 blue

The US Navy adopted the bolt-action 6mm Lee rifle in 1895; manufactured from 1896 by Winchester, it was used by both sailors and US Marines during the Boxer campaign of 1900, though production ceased in 1902. Its advantage over the Army's Krag-Jorgensen was that although both had a five-round magazine, only the Lee could be reloaded with a five-round clip, thus speeding up the process by vital seconds. (Photo Kristen Densmore; JS)

TOP **US Army infantrymen with the China Relief Expedition were armed with the .30-40cal Krag-Jorgensen rifle, adopted in the mid-1890s and already well proven in the Spanish-American War. Although the five-round magazine on the right side had to be loaded with individual rounds, this weapon was still a great improvement over the previously issued single-shot 'trapdoor' Springfield rifle; its ammunition used a smokeless propellant, avoiding the tell-tale cloud of powdersmoke that had both pinpointed and unsighted the user. (GL)**

ABOVE **Cavalry troopers were issued a shorter carbine version of the .30-40cal Krag-Jorgensen. Other advantages of this new generation of weapons was that the more powerful propellant gave a flatter trajectory and thus superior accuracy, and the smaller bullet allowed more of the lighter ammunition to be carried. (GL)**

jacket is trimmed with black mohair over the whole surface of the stand collar, down both front edges and round the skirt hem; the rank of captain in the line – the most senior officer to serve ashore during the China Relief Expedition – is indicated by the four gold cuff rings, and the silver eagles and anchors on each side of the collar. Ashore, naval officers adopted the practical canvas leggings worn by the US Army and Marine Corps.

C2: Musician, 14th US Infantry; campaign dress, 1900

During the course of the 1898 Spanish-American War the US Army adopted a khaki campaign uniform, though rushed early deliveries from a variety of manufacturers showed differences. This jacket is the M1899 type, with a rolled collar, and epaulets in the white branch-of-service color of the infantry. The drab 1899-pattern campaign hat has large wire gauze ventilators on each side of the crown. The weapon is the .30cal Krag-Jorgensen adopted in the mid 1890s, and the blue web Mills belt has double-banked loops to accommodate 90 rounds. Company musicians carried brass bugles with (for the infantry) white worsted cords. This soldier is in bivouac, and has dumped his marching pack and other field gear.

C3: Private, 5th US Artillery; campaign dress, 1900

Since he has laid aside his khaki jacket with red epaulets, nothing visibly identifies this gunner on the march across the plains as an artilleryman, though the M1887 khaki Mills belt has only a single bank of cartridge loops; the symbols of the branches of service were not at this date stenciled onto the haversack. In contrast to C2, he wears full marching gear: an M1885 haversack (with a tin cup looped to its fastening strap), an M1874 or 1879 canteen covered with pale drab canvas, and spare shirt, underwear, washing kit, tent-pegs and half-pole wrapped in a tent-half/blanket horseshoe roll slung around his torso.

D1: Major-General, US Army; Peking, 1900

After fighting ceased in Peking the American commanding officer, MajGen Adna Chaffee, exchanged his khaki field uniform and campaign hat for this M1898 dark blue double-breasted general officers' undress jacket; exact rank was indicated by the buttons spaced in groups of three, and shoulder straps with two silver stars on a black field. Matching dark blue trousers cut for riding, and an M1895 general officers' cap with black velvet band, complete this garrison uniform.

D2: Corporal, 14th US Infantry; winter dress, 1900/01

This corporal is in guard order during the cripplingly cold northern Chinese winter, for which he has been issued a flapped cap and big mittens in muskrat fur, as used by the US Army on the Plains since the late 1870s. The sky-blue heavy kersey overcoat has a long cape attaching under the deep fall collar; the cape is lined in dark blue for the infantry, and has a row of seven small brass buttons. Rank chevrons in dark blue with white chainstitch divisions are sewn to the coat cuffs, placed so as to be visible beneath the cape; the length of the coat almost hides the white trouser stripe of an infantry corporal. On sentry duty he carries his Krag with the bayonet fixed.

D3: First Sergeant, 6th US Cavalry, c.1900

The 'top soldier' of his troop wears immaculate undress uniform during an inspection. The crossed-sabers badge on his M1895 forage cap incorporates the regimental number and troop letter. The old-fashioned five-button M1883/90

Enlisted men of the Fifteenth US Infantry, dispatched to China for the first time in 1912, wore that year's new olive or khaki service uniforms with M1907 subdued bronze disk insignia on each side of the stand collar: on the right side the 'US' cypher, and on the left the Infantry rifles with the regimental number above and company letter below. (GL)

the adoption of campaign medals and ribbons from 1905 this practice declined. For full dress a sky-blue breast-and-shoulder cord with plaits and flounders was added to the uniform. The russet belt is fastened with an M1910 round brass 'US' clasp, and the weapon is the M1903 .30cal Springfield. Relatively inexpensive tailors in China permitted all ranks to procure and wear smart customized outfits long after the dress blue uniform became optional and all but disappeared with the outbreak of World War I.

E2: First Lieutenant, 15th US Infantry; full dress, 1912
A double-breasted dark blue wool frock coat with gilt buttons and gold cord shoulder knots was worn for full dress, with light blue collar and cuff facings for infantry officers. Rank appeared on the forearms: a plain sleeve indicated a second lieutenant, single-cord gold galloons ('chicken-guts') a first lieutenant, and so on up to the five galloons of the regiment's colonel. Crossed gold-wire embroidered rifles and a silver regimental number were applied in the lower angle of the lacing. Note the gold-and-light-blue full dress belt with its gilt and silver eagle plate.

E3: Lieutenant-Colonel, 15th US Infantry; undress, 1912
For everyday garrison wear and walking-out officers availed themselves of this stand-collar uniform jacket trimmed with black mohair. Shoulder straps indicated rank on a light blue background field: plain for second lieutenants, a single silver bar at each end for first lieutenants, and two silver bars for captains; gold oakleaves at each end for majors, silver oakleaves for lieutenant colonels, and a spread eagle for the regiment's colonel.

'sack coat' displays his rank on both upper sleeves, in single pieces of cavalry-yellow cloth divided into points-down chevrons with black chain-stitching, though in this case surmounted by the separate lozenge of first sergeant. The sky-blue trousers have the inch-wide yellow stripe of cavalry NCOs. The silver Maltese Cross award is a shooting badge; the carbine is the M1896 Krag.

E1: Battalion Sergeant-Major, 15th US Infantry; full dress, 1912
The full dress uniform prescribed at the end of 1902 remained regulation when the 15th Infantry marched into China a decade later. The gilt cap and collar badges are crossed rifles below the regimental number. This forage cap band, edged with sky-blue stripes top and bottom, was detachable for everyday dress. The tunic has six front buttons and three on the rear cuff seam. The closed stand collar is piped on all three edges with sky-blue, as are the epaulets and the top of the straight cuffs; the collar bears gilt 'US' cyphers ahead of the crossed rifles and number. The narrower rank insignia, now points-upward, are three chevrons and two 'rockers' in white, as are the inch-wide NCOs' trouser stripes. The length-of-service or 'hash' stripes to full width on both forearms are also in infantry white; originally these were color-coded to indicate the branch in which the man had served on active duty, but with

F1: Color-Sergeant, 15th US Infantry; summer service dress, 1912
At about the same time as the regiment took up duty in China a new stand-collar khaki service uniform became

After World War I bright gilt-finish collar insignia replaced the subdued versions: on the right side the national cypher and the regimental number, and on the left the Infantry rifles and the company letter. (GL)

The M1918 .30cal Browning Automatic Rifle (BAR), fed from 20-round clips, provided the US Army and Marines squad with automatic firepower from the end of World War I through the Korean War, and was also issued to the US Navy for use by boarding and landing parties. (NARA)

regulation, with M1907 bronze disk 'US' and branch-of-service insignia worn on the right and left collar respectively. A lightweight summer version of this M1912 uniform was provided for service in tropical climates or summer months, and in Tientsin men of the 15th regularly took advantage of local tailoring expertise to acquire custom-fitted jackets and tapered breeches of a distinctly 'golden' shade. Options for headgear were a khaki-covered cork summer helmet with a brown chinstrap, or the campaign hat – its crown now shaped into the four-dent 'Montana peak.' Subdued olive drab rank badges were worn above the elbows, here the three chevrons pointing upwards above a five-pointed star as prescribed for a color-sergeant. Each regiment had two of these non-commissioned officers; the senior of the pair carried the national colors on parade, his junior counterpart the blue silk regimental color; the butt of the staff was fitted into a heart-shaped brass holder suspended from a web strap secured under a separate web waist belt. Campaign ribbons and decorations would be worn above the left breast pocket on such occasions. In this image the color-sergeant is equipped for other duties, with two early clip pouches for the 1903 Springfield on his M1910 web belt.

F2: Chief Petty Officer, US Navy; summer shore party uniform, 1917

During World War I the US Navy remained on station in China ready for action. For chief petty officers the summer shore or landing party uniform consisted of a cap with white cover and black mohair band, bearing the badge of a silver fouled anchor with the gold letters 'USN' superimposed across the shank. A double-breasted coat with two rows of four gilt buttons had wide notched lapels and a single open pocket on the left breast; it was worn over a white shirt and black necktie. The rating badge was sewn on the left sleeve above the elbow for artificer rates, and on the right sleeve for the seaman branch, in navy-blue cloth on a white background; a chief displayed a spread eagle on an arc above a specialty device – here the crossed anchors of a boatswain – above three chevrons pointing downward. Blue length-of-service stripes, worn on the same sleeve as the rating during this period, indicated four years' service for each 'hash mark.' The outfit is completed here by black shoes, khaki leggings, and an M1912 web pistol belt supporting an M1911A1 semi-automatic in a russet leather

holster, and a two-clip web ammo pouch. Some sources show Navy use of the M1912 cavalry holster, hanging lower from the belt on its pivot-flap.

F3: First Sergeant, 15th US Infantry; walking-out dress, c.1930

In 1926 the Army adopted a smart new olive drab service uniform with a visored dress cap and open-lapel tunic for all ranks, worn with a white shirt and black necktie. The breeches-style trousers were retained, and were worn by the 15th with leg wraps (spiral puttees) that they bought at the neighboring British canteen. Men of the regiment had their walking-out uniforms privately tailor-made, and buttons of British manufacture were also used. A larger-than-regulation version of the regiment's enameled distinctive unit insignia was acquired, and placed on both the lower lapels. During this period some of the senior non-commissioned officers such as this first sergeant (designated by his three chevrons above a lozenge and two rockers) were long-service men, some of whom had reported to China when the regiment first arrived in 1912.

G1: Private First Class, US Marines Mounted Detachment; Peking, c.1933

The smart mounted detachment formed by the Legation Guard for ceremonial duties adapted the standard 'dress blues' by substituting riding breeches and hard-shell leggings for the issue sky-blue trousers and shoes, worn with dark blue or white 'covers' according to the season. The dark blue tunic bore red piping, gilt insignia and gold-on-red rank badges and service stripes; here an Expert Rifleman badge is worn below the ribbon of the Marine Good Conduct Medal. A white belt with a plain gilt plate was worn with blues by all personnel; the 'Horse Marines' carried an M1913 'Patton' saber. They rode McClellan saddles, with hooded stirrups embossed with 'USMC' on the front.

G2: US Marine winter cap badges, c.1935

Diamond-shaped metal badges were worn on winter headgear to identify subunits by color; the eagle, globe and anchor device was incorporated in both officers' bi-metal and enlisted bronze versions. A green background identified men serving with headquarters in Peking; white, the HQ Company of 4th Marines at Tientsin; red, Co A; pale blue, Co B; dark blue, Co C, and yellow, Company D.

G3: Major, 4th US Marines; service dress, winter 1935/36

The Marines' first forest-green service uniform dated from 1912; with this 1926 pattern officers wore bronze insignia, the M1935 Sam Browne belt, and usually a green vizored cap with a quatrefoil knot on the top surface of the crown, but in the Chinese winter this 'Mongolian piss-cutter' was substituted. Made of lambswool (or allegedly, cat fur), this headgear was unique to the 'Old Asiatic Station'; here it bears the white-backed badge of the Tientsin headquarters.

H1: Able Seaman, US Navy Yangtze Patrol, 1930s

The everyday working dress of a light blue-gray chambray shirt and dark blue dungarees was a utilitarian outfit for landing and boarding parties, with the substitution of the M1917A1 steel helmet in Navy gray finish for the sailor's 'dixie cup' hat, and the addition of web leggings and combat equipment. This 'gob' provides the party's main firepower, with an M1918 .30cal Browning Automatic Rifle rigged for firing from the hip. The M1918 BAR 'rifleman's magazine belt' has a metal cup on the right side for supporting the butt; it also carries a holstered .45cal pistol for self-defense, two pistol clip pouches, and four magazine pouches each holding two 20-round BAR magazines.

H2: Campaign medals

(a) US Army China Campaign Medal – authorized January 11, 1905, for service with the Peking Relief Expedition between June 20, 1900 and May 27, 1901; this bears the Chinese imperial dragon on the obverse.
(b) US Navy and Marine Corps China Relief Expedition Medal – authorized June 27, 1908, for Navy and Marine personnel serving between May 24, 1900 and May 27, 1901; this bears a Peking city gate and an imperial dragon.

During 1932 the Thirty-First Infantry were also deployed to China from their base in the Philippines at the time of tension following the outbreak of fighting between the Chinese and Japanese in Manchuria and the Japanese landing at Shanghai. Their distinctive unit insignia, approved on February 29, 1924, featured a polar bear, reflecting the regiment's service in Siberia at the close of World War I. The regimental motto 'Pro Patria' – For Our Country – was indicative of the unit's spirit even though it had hardly set foot in the United States for much of its existence. (GL)

In February 1925 the Fifteenth Infantry was authorized a distinctive unit insignia in white and dark blue enamel on bronze with a gilt 'mountain' centrally. The imperial dragon was a reference to the regiment's service against the Boxers, and the motto 'Can Do' was originally a phrase in so-called pidgin English – a further indication of the unit's long association with China. The insignia was placed on the lower lapels of the open-collar service coat and on the campaign hat; locally made versions were larger than regulation size. (GL)

(c) US Navy and Marine Corps Yangtze Service Medal – authorized April 28, 1930, for Navy and Marine personnel serving in Shanghai or the Yangtze Valley; this bears a Chinese junk on the obverse.
(d) US Navy and Marine Corps China Service Medal – authorized August 23, 1940, for Navy and Marine personnel serving during operations in China from July 7, 1937 to September 7, 1939.

H3: Captain, 4th US Marines; Shanghai, summer 1937

Uniform Regulations, US Marine Corps, 1937 prescribed for officers a summer field uniform consisting of a starched khaki cotton shirt bearing small-size insignia of rank (two silver bars for captains) on both collar points; a field scarf (necktie); and khaki cotton breeches secured below the knee and with reinforcing along the lower inseam if so desired. Brown leather high-topped shoes and matching shell puttees (hard gaiters) in USMC Shade 141 were worn, the latter fastening either by straps and clips or by laces. The web pistol belt supported by suspenders carried a holstered M1911A1 .45cal Colt semi-automatic – here, hanging low in the cavalry-pattern M1912 holster with pivot-tab and leg strap, and with a long cord lanyard worn around the torso. The belt also supports a double pistol clip pouch, first aid pocket and canteen. Officers might also carry field-glasses in a leather case with a shoulder sling, and a compass secured by a heavy chain; such affectations as bamboo-and-leather canes were private purchase items. Headgear could be either the steel helmet; the brimmed campaign hat with eagle, globe and anchor insignia fixed in front and an intermixed gold-and-scarlet cord terminating in two 'acorns,' with a narrow leather strap worn around the back of the head; or this fiber tropical helmet.

INDEX

Figures in **bold** refer to illustrations.

Abarerda, USS 24
aircraft, US 41
Albany, USS 5, 6
Alice Dollar, USS 38
Armstrong, Capt James 9, 10
Arrow War (1856–60) 3, 8
artillery **9, 10, 15**, 16, 21, **22**
Ashevelli, USS 6
Augusta, USS 7

Bainbridge, USS **37**
Baltimore, USS 5
Barrier Forts **3**, 8, **8**–10
'Bataan Death March' 36
Battle of Lugou Bridge (1937) 7, 34, 35, 39
Belnap, Cdre Roger C. 4–5
Boston, USS 5, **22**
Boxer Rising, the (1900) 5, **10**, 10–22
'Brown Water Navy,' the 37–40
Butler, BrigGen Smedley 7, 16, 34

Cabell, Capt De Rosey C. 18, 21
Chaffee, Gen Adna 5, 17, 19, 20, **20**, 21, 22
Chang Tso-lin ('the Tiger of the North') 39
Chennault, Capt Claire L. 40, 41
Chiang Kai-shek 7, 35, 39, 40, 41
China Relief Expedition 17–22
Chinese Communist Party (CCP) 6
chronology 4–8
Chu Te 7, 39
Colt .236cal 'potato-digger' machineguns 12
Colt double-action revolvers 18
Curtis-Wright P-40B fighter aircraft 41

Daggett, Col A. S. 18
Daly, Pte Daniel 16

First American Volunteer Group 40–42
'Flying Tigers,' the 40–42
Foote, Commander Andrew H. **3, 8**, 9, 10
Foreign Powers Expeditionary Force 5

Galveston, USS **37**
garrisons (1900–1941) 22–36
Gaselee, LtGen Alfred 17, 19, 20
Gatling guns **22**
Gauss, Gen Clarence 35
Gold Star, USS 6

Hall, Capt N. H. 12, 14
Hall, Capt Newt T. 15, 16
Hartford, USS 5
Houston, USS 39
humanitarian aid 39
Huron, USS 6

insignia **33, 45, 47**

Japanese invasion of China 7–8, 33–34, 39

Krag rifles **18, 44, C2** (29, 44)
Krupp guns **9**
Kuomintang Party (KMT) 6, 7, 33, 35, 37, 39

Levant, USS 4, 8, 9
'Literal Study Society' 5
Logan, USS 24
Luzon, USS 40

M1816 Springfield muskets **A2** (26, 43)
M1863 Springfield muskets **A3** (26, 43)
M1895 Lee rifles **43, B1** (28, 43)
M1903 Springfield rifles **E1** (31, 45)
M1911A1 semi-automatic **F2** (32, 46)
M1918 .30cal Browning Automatic Rifles **46, H1** (34, 47)
MacDonald, Sir Claude 11–12, 14
Manchu dynasty 3, 10, 11, 23
Mao Tse-tung 6, 39
'Marco Polo Bridge Incident' (1937) 7, 34, 35, 39
Martini-Henry .455in rifles **6**
Mauser rifles **10**
Maxim machineguns **10**, 12
May Fourth movement 6
McCalla, Capt Bowman 5, 12, 13
'Mekden Incident' (1931) 7
Merry Moller, USS **41**
Mindanao, USS 40
missionaries 11
Mississippi, USS 4
Monocacy, USS 5
Myers, Capt John 'Handsome Jack' 5, 12, **12**, 13, 14, 15

Nanking Conference (1911) 5
Newark, USS 12

Oahu, USS 40
Opium Wars (1839–42, 1856–60) 3, 8
Oregon, USS 5, 12

Panay, USS 8, 35
Pearl Harbour, attack on (1941) 8, 36
Pei Tsang 18–20
Peking 5, 6, 7, **11**, 11–16, 20–22, **21**, 24, 34
Penguin, USS 38
Pigeon, USS 38
Pittsburgh, USS 7
Portsmouth, USS **3**, 4, **8**, 9

Rainbow, USS 5–6
Raleigh, USS 5
'Rape of Nanking' (1937) 39
Reilly, Capt Henry J. 18, 20
revolvers **18**, 21
rifles **6, 10, 18, 43, 44, 46, B1** (28, 43), **C2** (29, 44), **E1** (31, 45), **H1** (34, 47)

Sacramento, USS 6
San Jacinto, USS 4, 9
Saratoga, USS 5, **37**

Savage-Landor, Henry 22, 23
Seymour, Admiral Sir Edward 14, 17
Shanghai 4, 5, 6, 7, **7, 8**, 24, 34–35, 36, **36**
Sino-Japanese War (1937–45) 7, 34–35
St Louis, USS 4
Sun Ch'uan-fang ('the Nanking Warlord') 37
Sun Yat-sen 5, 6, 23, 37

Taiping Rebellion (1850–64) 8, 10
Taku Forts **9**, 17–18
Tientsin 6, 7, 8, 12, 13, 16, 17–18, **23**, 24, 33, 34, **34**, 36
Treaty of Versailles (1919) 6
Tulsa, USS 7
Tutulia, USS 40
Tzu Hsi, Dowager Empress 11

uniforms 5, 7, **18, 19, 20, 21, 22, 24, 34, 35, 36, A** (26, 43), **B** (28, 43), **C** (29, 43–44), **D** (30, 44–45), **E** (31, 45), **F** (32, 45–46), **G** (33, 46–47), **H** (34, 47)
US Forces *see also* uniforms; weapons
   Boxer Rising (1900) 5, **10**, 10–22
   the 'Brown Water Navy' 37–40
   China Relief Expedition 17–22
   Chinese Regiments **6**
   chronology 4–8, **7**
   the 'Flying Tigers' 40–42
   garrisons (1900–1941) 22–36
   humanitarian aid 39
   insignia **33, 45, 47**
   medals **H2** (34, 47)
   Pei Tsang and Yang Tsun 18–20
   Peking 5, 6, 7, **11**, 11–16, 20–22, **21**, 24, 34
   Taku Forts **9**, 17–18
   Tientsin 6, 7, 8, **9**, 12, 13, 16, 17–18, **23**, 24, 33, 34, **34**, 36
   US Army (1912–1938) 23–25, 33–34
   US Marines (1927–41) 34–36
   World War I (1914–1918) 33

Wachusett, USS 4
Wake, USS 40
'Warlord Period' 37
weapons
   artillery **9, 10, 15**, 16, 21, **22**
   machineguns **10**, 12
   muskets **A2** (26, 43), **A3** (26, 43)
   revolvers **18**, 21,
   rifles **6, 10, 18, 43, 44, 46, B1** (28, 43), **C2** (29, 44), **E1** (31, 45), **H1** (34, 47)
World War I (1914–1918) 33
Wu Pie-fu ('the Jade Marshal') 37, 39
Wyoming, USS 4–5

Yang Tsun 18–20
Yangtze Patrol, the 37–40
Yi Ho Tuan movement *see* Boxer Rising, the (1900)